GROWING UP BUSKE

GROWING UP BUSKE

A COLLECTION OF MEMORIES

MARK EDWARD BUSKE

For Mom and Dad and for Sis

And for the wonderful circle of supportive friends, who deserve a nickel for every time you've heard my stories.

You've enriched my life beyond measure.

That's me and my bow-tie in my first-grade portrait. Even then, I had plenty to say and stories to tell.

CONTENTS

TO THE READER

At the age of seventy, my dad sat down at his desk with a yellow pad of paper and began writing stories—stories of growing up on a farm and attending a one-room schoolhouse. (Dad graduated top in his class. The only other eighth grader came in second!) He wrote of his life in the Army, of meeting and marrying my mom, and raising a family on a farm of his own. He spent the next eleven years adding to his book of stories, sharing them with anyone who would listen.

It was New Year's Day in 2014, when my folks, Sis, and I had our final lunch together. (We grew up calling the noon meal *dinner* and the evening meal *supper*. Lunch was served when you had family over on Saturday night, around 9 o'clock, but I digress.) Dad passed away suddenly later that day, and the job of telling stories passed to me. Initially, writing these stories down was a way to grieve him.

The project grew and the stories kept coming, especially on evenings Mom and I spent at her new home "in town." Life on the farm without Dad wasn't the same, and she'd grown tired of mowing the grass. Then, on New Year's Day, just six years after Dad, Sis and I lost Mom. Our folks had done everything together for sixty years; I guess we shouldn't have been surprised.

In these pages, you'll find stories that celebrate our family, memories of what seem like more innocent years, and tales of growing up in rural Illinois. They are a collection, some from those yellow pad pages of Dad's, some from the quiet evenings reminiscing with Mom, most from the memories still clear in my mind.

I hope these tales will prompt your own good memories and stories, and I encourage you to share them with those you love.

Mark Edward Buske

August 2021

PART I

IN THE BEGINNING

That's me, Cowboy Mark, riding our pony named Rusty, with the old farmhouse in the background. I was bucked off just after this photo was taken. I don't recall ever riding Rusty again.

1

THE OLD HOUSE, PART I

I AM AN OLD MAN.

I know this because I carry a handkerchief in my back pocket, a white piece of fabric carefully starched, folded, and ironed. I take this piece of fabric out of my pocket to wipe off my glasses or blow my nose, then return it to its holding place.

This is what old men do.

Old men also tell tales of growing up. These are mine, and most of them are true.

I wasn't born in a barn, though Mom still managed to ask a million times if I had been. I'd do something foolish, and she'd tease, "Hey, Schnicklefritz, close the door! Were you born in a barn?" I never did understand why she said that. After all, when I arrived on the seventh of November 1964,

I'm pretty sure she was there. And we were at Staunton Hospital in Staunton, Illinois, not in a barn.

And, yes, Mom called me "Schnicklefritz" and "Muscles" (pronounced "mus kles"), both of which were terms of endearment. When I heard her call out, "Mark Edward," however, it was not so dear; it meant I was in trouble. Those stories I'll share later.

Mom and Dad had been married ten years when I came along, a package deal. They got a baby, a new furnace, and a bathtub. I guess the hospital was running a special.

You see, the old farmhouse they were renting had an upstairs sink (pronounced "zink," at least by Mom) and a toilet, but no tub. Fred Dzengolewski, who owned the old house, as well as the 170 acres that Dad was farming, bought a cast-iron claw-foot tub. Since it clearly wouldn't fit up the staircase, they removed an upstairs window, rigged a set of ropes and pulleys, and hauled that heavy bathtub up and over the front porch.

Now my folks had a real tub to bathe their number one son in. But I don't really remember that fancy bathtub. What I do remember is the tin wash tub near the kitchen zink, I mean, sink, which Mom used to bathe me in on Saturday nights, whether I needed it or not.

The other part of the deal was an oil-burning furnace. Before I came along, Dad used a wood-burning stove to heat the oldest part of the house—a two-room cabin with a small attic that was used to store potatoes, onions, and the occasional snake—and a coal-burning stove to heat the front portion of the house—a Victorian addition of two rooms over two rooms, with a fancy front porch just large enough to pull a bathtub over.

Anyway, with a baby coming, Dad got permission from Fred Dzengolewski to update the heating system, then got his brother-in-law, Erwin Smith, to help him install it. Erwin was married to Dad's oldest sister, Erna. She was named for her grandmothers, Ida Johnson Engelmann and Albertina Dagler Buske. Thus, my aunt, who was also my godmother, was called Ida Albertina Erna, but only if you wanted to make her mad. To the family, she was just known as Erna.

And so, my folks had indoor plumbing, heat, and a kid. Eighteen months later, they had two kids, thanks to the arrival of my baby sister, Janet Lynn. The old house was now full.

Janet and I slept in bunk beds in the room behind the kitchen, the "cabin" portion of the old house. Mom and Dad slept in one of the two first-floor rooms, the "Victorian" part of the house. My earliest memories are of the two of us climbing out of our bunk beds and into Mom and Dad's bed. There, Dad would imitate the birds by whistling their calls: "Whip-poor-will. Whip-poor-will." We felt safe. And loved.

2

THE WELL HOUSE

THERE WERE three wells on our farm. The one we used for drinking water was right in the center of the homestead. Our lane ended just past it at the tool shed, and a brick sidewalk led away from it toward the old house.

That well had a hand pump and a tin cup that hung from a wire. The pump sat on a concrete pad to cover the well's opening, and a little house built from cinder blocks, complete with a door and three windows, surrounded it. The well house is where Mom kept some gardening tools and Dad kept his beer.

It was also a gathering place.

When Sis and I were really little, we'd play hide-and-seek with Jay, our neighbor's teenage boy, who was hired as an occasional farm hand. Jay could typically find us in one of two places: in the playroom closet of the old house, or hiding among the gardening tools in the well house.

We didn't drink Dad's beer while we hid, I promise.

In the spring, one of my chores was to water the tomato and pepper plants in the garden. My job was to pump a bucket full of water, carry it past the chicken house to the garden, and use a tin can—bottom punched with holes—as a sprinkler. One can of water per plant when they were little, two after they'd grown. I tended to splash more water on my pants than I did on the plants.

Those five-gallon buckets were heavy.

Around the time I was eight, the well house had become a backdrop for batting practice. Dad stood just across the lane, tossing pitches my way. I stood by the well house, swinging at the air, letting the door stop the ball.

I may have been a lousy batter, but Dad was a great pitcher. Together, we never broke a window.

In summer, we'd pull out of the field and park the tractors by the tool shed, then pump a drink of cool water from the well. That tin cup was passed around, then filled again. Sometimes I'd pour the water over my arms to remove the dust, especially when we baled straw.

Long after he retired, Dad decided to try his hand at painting. Inspired by watching artist Bob Ross on TV reruns, he painted a beach scene on the well house door. He even painted a V in the sky, to represent a bird.

It's funny, what we remember.

I've kept a number of things from the farm to remind me of those days. Wish I'd kept that tin cup. I can still taste the tin on my lips

3

THE OLD HOUSE, PART II

THE BUNK BED arrangement in the room I shared with Sis
didn't last long. In the first place, the second room of the
"cabin" portion of the house wasn't really a bedroom. It
wasn't really anything specific, for that matter.

The room held a large chest freezer (the first thing Mom
and Dad bought when they moved to the farm in 1956. It
was in the basement of the "new house when we left the
farm in 2014, still running)." The room also held an
antique china cabinet purchased for five dollars from a
woman in Troy, not long after Mom and Dad brought the
freezer. It was the room where Mom ironed while she
watched soap operas on a twelve-inch black-and-white television. To top it off, the room had a large closet Dad built
using fake wood paneling popular in the late '60s, that
same closet where Sis and I could be found when playing
hide-and-seek.

The room contained, and was used for, all these things, but it wasn't really a bedroom. So, the bunk beds were separated and carried up the stairs of the Victorian part of the house, then placed on either end of one of the second floor's two rooms. Now Sis and I slept upstairs, our folks slept downstairs, and the stairs themselves became a playroom. We discovered how far toy trucks could travel if pushed down the stairs. And beach balls. And Slinkys. We tried the stairs while on our Romper Stompers, which we'd seen on "Romper Room" on Mom's black-and-white TV.

Soon enough, our toy box was moved to the room with the freezer, the china cabinet, and the ironing board. The room took on a new name: the playroom. And Mom announced a new rule. Toys did not leave the playroom. Period.

Now, the playroom had most everything, but it didn't have a telephone. Our only phone hung on the wall in the kitchen, and it was set up as a "party line"—meaning we shared the line with our neighbors. Mrs. Weber from the farm next door never called; if she needed something, she simply walked over to our farm. Old Mrs. Conrad, who lived a little farther away, called our home all the time, looking for her cats. I think poor Mrs. Conrad had lost more than her cats.

As for me, I only recall using that phone once. Dad and I were home alone, and he was trying to repair an old CASE planter, or an old CASE three-bottom plow. All of our farm equipment was CASE, and in constant need of repair. In this instance, the implement in question needed welding, which required the help of our local welder. Rather than take me along, he gave me the welder's phone number and told me to call in case of an emergency. Then Dad left. I guess I felt his leaving was an emergency, because I phoned the welder before Dad even arrived at his shop.

He never left me again.

Well, not on the farm. But that's a story for later.

4

THE TOOLSHED

WE CALLED IT THE TOOLSHED. The folks who built it probably called it the carriage house. A pair of large wooden doors hung on either end of the building, with space behind each set for a buggy or a car. In the center was a room large enough for Dad's collection of hand tools, all the items a farmer needs in organized displays. That room was half the depth of the two garage spaces, and the remaining space behind the room was used as a corn crib.

Dad kept a scoop shovel in the corn crib. The crib itself had two small doors, one near the peak of the roof, where Dad would place an auger and shoot ears of corn into the crib. The other small door was level with the wooden floor. It was just big enough for me to crawl into so that I could kick down the remaining ears of corn that had gotten stuck in the corners and crevices of the crib.

When I was a little older and slightly stronger, I could use the shovel to scoop the corn myself, dropping it into metal buckets that I'd carry to the pig lot. I'd dump the corn on the ground for the piggies, then run like heck to get out of their way.

One harvest season, the old CASE combine was giving Dad particular heck, and he'd parked it in front of the toolshed and placed a tarp underneath. He was on his back, deep under the belly of the combine, muttering his share of cuss words, when he called me over.

"Mark, get me a wrench."

I looked over the items in the organized display and grabbed what I thought was a wrench.

"No, son, a wrench. Get me a wrench."

I selected another tool, which clearly turned out not to be a wrench.

"Dammit, Mark. You don't know which one is a wrench?"

I learned what a wrench was. I also learned to hand Dad the tools and let him do the repair work, a pattern he and I followed from then on.

Truth be told, Dad rarely cussed, and usually only when we were loading hogs for market. If you've ever loaded hogs up a wooden chute and onto a waiting truck, then you've probably said a few choice words of your own.

Most times, Dad was in a good mood and always found time to play. For instance, there was a basketball hoop over the central door of the toolshed and Dad, Sis, and I would "shoot hoops" on summer evenings. There was never a net, so if I did make a basket, I'd make my own "swoosh" noise.

I bought my first car the summer before my freshman year of college. It was a 1976 silver Caprice Classic with balding tires and a leaking roof. Dad called it "The Silver Streak" because I drove too fast. I called it "The Grey Goose." I think I paid $800 for it; I know I thought I was hot stuff.

The Grey Goose sat outside most of that freshman year while I continued to live at home on the farm. By my sophomore year, Dad agreed to park his truck outside, and gave me the carriage house garage on the right-hand side of the toolshed. It was a tight fit; a full-size Chevrolet was far bigger than the horse buggies that once occupied the space. I had to back out for anyone else to get in.

When parked inside, the car was surrounded by Dad's memorabilia: every license plate he ever had hung on the wall, in order of the year issued. Every hub cap he found along the side of State Highway 4, which divided our 170 acres more or less in half, hung on the opposite wall. A railroad track, used as a coal line in those days and a bike path now, divided the farm at a cross section. Lots of vehicles traveled too quickly down Highway 4, hit those tracks, and left an offering for Dad's hub cap collection.

Those old license plates brought a pretty penny at the public auction we held after Dad passed, as did most of the junk he collected over his lifetime. And some items that were prized by him brought nothing at all. But the oddest thing that we pulled from the toolshed and sold at the auction was a large Santa blow mold. We had loads of wooden outdoor Christmas decorations: elves, reindeer, even baby Jesus, but there was never a plastic Santa in our annual display. For years, Mom wondered where that Santa came from, and how it landed in our toolshed.

Perhaps it fell off a speeding truck when it crossed the railroad tracks.

5

BREAK A LEG!

THAT PARTY LINE phone in the kitchen wasn't our only way to communicate with the outside world, though it was the fastest. Another way was to stick our heads out the kitchen door and holler. Lines like, "Dinner's ready," or "Supper's ready," or "Someone's on the phone for you" were yelled frequently. Sometimes, just someone's name. Like the time Mom hollered for me, and I didn't answer.

You see, even as a little kid, I liked to work in the garden. We typically had two. The small one by the chicken house held things like strawberries and rhubarb. In the big garden, we planted tomatoes, squash, peppers, and potatoes. That garden was bordered by a small grape arbor and a gooseberry bush on the west, and rows of zinnias and sweet corn on the east. The sweet corn rows often gave way to field corn rows, and that's where the hollering comes in.

I was out hoeing the rows of sweet corn, the stalks as tall as me, and continued into the field corn, which was even taller. Mom hollered for me and I didn't come. She must have called a number of times, and when I didn't answer and couldn't be seen, she phoned Aunt Eileen to come over and help look for me. About that time, I came walking out of the cornfield, hoe in hand. According to Mom, I had walked to the railroad track and back, hoeing the corn as I went. Scared that poor woman to death.

I guess I scared my folks often growing up. Hernia surgery at St. Louis Children's Hospital before I was a year old, noted vision loss at an early age with glasses soon to follow, a tumor removed from my lower jaw line when only a baby, speech therapy in first grade to fix my R's and S's. (I'll bet they're sorry that got fixed. I haven't shut up since.)

But the scariest incident for my folks must have been when I broke my leg. I had just turned seven, and was spending a November day at Aunt Eileen and Uncle Les's farm. Quite a large crew was helping Les butcher, including my folks, while a number of us kids played in the yard. Seems like we were always at someone's farm, butchering a cow or a pig or making summer sausage or blood sausage or head cheese. Buske, after all, translates from German to English as "will eat anything"—or words to that effect.

But back to the broken leg. I was hanging—literally—with the rest of the kids, climbing on to a large wooden spool used by the county to store electrical wire. That spool was stationed at the base of a tree, beneath a rope. I climbed up on the spool and grabbed for the rope.

I missed.

I spent Thanksgiving and Christmas in the hospital in Staunton, Illinois. Highland Hospital was only a fifteen-minute drive from Uncle Les's farm, but both Janet and I were born in Staunton Hospital, and my folks decided to take me back to the scene of the crime. I was placed across their laps, riding in our Ford pick-up on Highway 4, a 40-minute ride past our own farm, over Interstate 55, and over at least four rough railroad crossings. I cried at every bump.

Body casts are not meant for seven-year-olds. Mine started at my left ankle and ended at my belly button, wrapping all of my left leg and most of my middle in plaster. Yes, they left the appropriate holes in the cast. And the cast came after a week of having first both legs, then just the left, suspended in the air. Traction, I think they called it. Pain in the, uh, broken leg, if you ask me.

I had my coloring books to keep my mind off the pain. And the kid in the next bed, who would slap me every night to get me to stop crying. He and I did not exchange addresses when he left. And I had Mom, who slept on an outdoor lounge chair, the kind with the wide plastic webbing, beside my bed each night, until the nurses made her stay home.

I took my turn in that same lounge chair, once I finally got to go home. It was set up in the toy room, that second room of the "cabin" portion of the old house, and that's where I stayed most of the day. I spent many hours trying to do the homework Mrs. Dolores Hoge, my second-grade teacher, brought me, and watching the soap operas on that black-and-white TV while Mom ironed.

I got back to school around Valentine's Day.

If you think breaking your leg is scary, try handing out Valentine's cards to every one of your second-grade class-mates while on crutches. Now that's frightening.

NORTH BARN

FARM KIDS LEARN at an early age not to name the livestock.

Naming the animals turns them into pets. Dogs, cats, even horses make great pets. Cows, pigs, and chickens make great meals. No one wants to sit down to dinner and discover that the main dish is—or was—a beloved animal that they played with just a few hours earlier.

Despite that rule, I named our newest delivery of baby calves. I called them Mandy, Candy, Randy, Sandy, Dandy, Andy, and George. These seven brown-eyed cuties came from my Uncle Gerp Schumacher, whose first name was really Gervase, and whose occupation was dairy farmer.

Dairy farming must have been even more demanding than hog farming during my childhood, because the seven Schumacher cousins would always leave family reunions early to milk the cows. Our pigs neither needed nor wanted attention, so we stayed at family reunions through the evening meal and Dad would keep telling stories and drinking one more beer until, well, the cows came home.

Anyway, each fall, Uncle Gerp would set aside six or seven young male calves to sell to my dad, and that's when the fun began. Every morning and every night, Sis and I would bottle feed the baby calves, using powdered milk and really large plastic baby bottles. Picture a container large enough to feed an infant Paul Bunyan, and you'll get the idea.

The calves were housed in a section of the north barn, one of the three original barns on our farm. It was the largest of the three and had two haylofts, three brick-lined grain bins, sleeping quarters for the cows, and an area once used for storing hay wagons. Dad gated off that area, and it was now home to Sandy, Mandy, George, and the rest of the crew.

So, with our pant legs tucked firmly into our rubber boots, and with a baby bottle filled with warm milk, Sis and I would troop out to the holding area with Dad (who could hold a bottle in each hand), thrust the nipples between the bars of the steel gate, then hold on as best we could while the little guys did their thing. Once the first four were fed, we'd start the process all over again.

By winter, the calves had free reign of the north barn as well as the whole north lot, fenced so that neither they nor the hogs could escape. Now my job was to climb up to the barn's loft and toss down a bale of hay, break down the bale, and pitch it into a large wooden feeder stuck in the middle of the north lot.

Filling the wood trough with hay seems an easy enough job for a little kid, but it was invariably muddy during the winter months. So, on more than one occasion, one of my boots would remain stuck in the muck while my stocking foot danced in the air.

Once that chore was done, I would return to the loft and kick down a bale or two of straw. Dad would spread it throughout the barn where the growing cattle slept. It looked sort of like a nativity scene, only without a baby. Or shepherds. Or angels.

Goodnight, Sandy. Goodnight, Randy. Goodnight, George. Sleep tight. Butchering day is long after Christmas.

WE WERE HEROES

So, we stuck both hands over the hole and saved the boat from sinking. Or so we believed....

That's a great line to the end of a story, but let's go back to the beginning.

The Buske family was once again on the road, this time for a weekend trip to sunny Branson, Missouri. We'd packed our suitcases, camp stove, ice chest, and a couple paper bags of groceries, into the Ford du jour, and we were heading southwest on I-55. Our first stop: a roadside entertainment, billed as A Real Western Day's Experience.

Dad parked the car, bought four tickets, then guided us on to a small train, one that ran on tires rather than tracks. The disguised tram took us into the rolling Missouri hills, where—sure 'nuff—a smattering of old-timey buildings lined a single, dusty street.

I was almost six, Sis would have just turned four, so memories of our escapades until the gun fight are fuzzy. From the gun shots on, the picture is much clearer.

Two men—one good guy, one bad—stand on either end of that single street, aiming at one another and talking loudly. Gunshots go off, and the bad guy drops to the ground. A fellow wearing a big gold star—clearly the sheriff—walks over to where our family is standing with the gathered crowd. He taps my dad's shoulder and asks him to help move the body out of sight of the "chil'ren and womenfolk."

Sis and I take it all in, believing every moment to be real. Sis begins crying, and then I begin crying, and soon we're really bawling our eyes out. Dad soon appears, alive and well, and Mom dries our tears. The four of us mosey over to the dressed-up train, and we ride back to civilization.

But the day's entertainment isn't over.

The next stop is a drive-through Wild Animal Safari, a tourist, uh, destination that is still in operation today. Probably with the same animals.

Dad pretends to be our safari guide, and Mom pretends to be afraid every time the animals get close. "Vernon! Vernon! Pull up! Aaaagh!" Mom does a convincing job of being afraid. Sis and I believe the whole show.

Next, the emus stick their heads directly into the open windows of our non-air-conditioned Ford while we laugh and laugh and take pictures with the Kodak. Then Mom swats them away while trying not to mess up her beehive hairdo. That's her signal to Dad that our safari is over, so he pulls back on to the highway, and we continue the journey.

Now we arrive in 1960s Branson, home of Presley's Country Jubilee, the Baldknobbers Theater, and the brand-new Silver Dollar City amusement park. And not much else. Hotels don't exist. Motels do, and we rent a motel room right downtown, near Main Street, just a short walk from Lake Taneycomo.

And we're finally back to the beginning of this story.

We have supper, which I imagine was hamburgers grilled on the Coleman camp stove and eaten with freshly sliced tomatoes and potato chips on a picnic bench somewhere on the motel grounds. The four of us are seated on a small excursion boat with a white canopy, enjoying the views of Lake Taneycomo. It's near the end of our little trip, and the captain calls out over the hand-held mic, "Gosh, folks, the boat has sprung a leak."

Sure 'nuff, right in the center of our little rig is a drain with water rising out of it. A fountain, if you will, squirting a trickle of water.

"Thank goodness you kids are on board! Put your fingers in the hole and stop the water or we'll sink!" Sis and I skill-fully cover the hole, but water keeps coming.

"Use your whole hands, now," the captain instructs. "Both of you. C'mon, quick!"

Magically, the massive trickle stops. Sis and I, barely four and almost six, save the day. We were heroes.

Or so we believed.

That's the wonderful thing about childhood. We're super-heroes one moment and wide-eyed with innocence the next. We cry unabashedly and laugh whole-heartedly. We believe, and trust, and love.

8

THE CHICKEN HOUSE

THE ORIGINAL PLAN for our farm may have called for a chicken coop of some sort, but the Dzengolewski family never got around to building one. Perhaps their chickens roamed free around the north and south barns, or near the well house, or in and out of the little coal shed.

No matter. Not long after my folks left the Army and moved in with Grandma and Grandpa Buske—the summer of 1956—Dad got permission from the farm's owner, Fred Dz+eleven more letters, to add a coop and raise chickens.

Uncle Les and Dad built the coop themselves, a tin structure about 20-foot long, 10-foot wide, the center just high enough for a short man of German heritage (Dad) to stand up fully, which meant the entry door was short and required folks to duck before entering.

I suppose there is some humor in having to duck to enter a house meant for chickens, but I digress….

The interior included a room just for hatchlings. Every spring we'd ride in the truck to Edwardsville and buy 40 or 50 baby chicks. They came in a giant cardboard box, poked with many an air hole. Once we were home, Dad would carefully place the box in the center of the hatchling room. Sis and I would then stand in the main room of the coop and peek through the knot holes of the boards framing the hatching space. Finally, delaying the suspense no longer, Dad would release the chicks and they'd scatter to the four corners of the little room. We'd laugh and smile and wonder at the sight and sound of all those baby chicks!

Now, a good job for a little kid is to collect the eggs from those grown chicks. But this little kid only liked them as babies; grown chickens pecked and squawked and generally scared the heck out of me. I did not like the chickens, and they weren't fond of me, either.

Nor were the geese, for that matter. Or the ducks. Or the guineas, which slept on the lower branches of the two giant elm trees along the brick sidewalk—the path that led from the old house, past the well house, and to the lane. I had to pass them all, crossing the lane and walking past the rhubarb and strawberry patch to get to the chicken house.

Once, a mother goose chased me out to the edge of the cornfield, where Dad had set up an electric fence. I ran away from that goose and right into the electrified line, giving me a nice zing across my young belly.

Mom didn't get any eggs that day

9

HUNTING RABBITS

"What rabbit, Mommy?"

"Mark, the one running across the field. There goes another. Can't you see them?"

"No, Mommy. I don't see no rabbits."

I rubbed my eyes and looked again. Still no rabbits. Just a big, green field, and the railroad tracks beyond.

I rubbed my eyes a lot, or so Mom told me. I drew outside the lines in my coloring books. I tripped over cracks in the sidewalk. I failed to catch the balls Dad tossed to me. I managed to get through kindergarten thanks only to the kindness of my teacher, Miss Korsmeyer. Because, truth be told, I wasn't noticing the giant letters above the chalkboard, nor was I writing my name very clearly, or succeeding at much of anything.

I simply couldn't see—especially the rabbits chasing each other across the field.

Dr. Rosenthal was a nice man. His father, also known as Dr. Rosenthal, was an "eye doctor," an optometrist with an office in Highland. His son, Robert, had followed in his father's footsteps, and sometime around 1970—first grade for me, with Mrs. Gentry—I had my first appointment with Dr. Bob.

"One, or two." I was six. One or two meant something very different to me. But Dr. Bob asked again. "One, or two." "Two, I think." "Good. Now, three, or four?"

I saw Dr. Bob every year after that.

During second grade with Mrs. Hoge, during third grade with Mrs. Boglo—every year was the same. A desk up front so that I could see the board. A new prescription from Dr. Bob, so that I could see the rabbits. And the cracks in the sidewalk.

By fourth grade—with Miss Fuller, my favorite—I had the routine down pat. Desk up front, on the left-hand side of the classroom, because my right eye was dominant. "Two, not one," and Dr. Bob would dial in a stronger prescription. New prescription lenses in old frames, because we didn't always have the money for new ones. I could catch more of what was going on around me, and occasionally, even catch one of the softballs Dad tossed my way.

So, Dad decided it was time to take his number one son hunting. Rabbit hunting, to be exact. He started me out on target practice, aiming a BB gun at a stack of beer cans. Could have been soda cans, but who could tell from across the yard? Not me.

First shot, I missed. Second shot, I hit the chicken house, which, to my credit, was at least in the same direction as the stack of cans.

Third shot, I missed again; but hey, Charlie the beagle finally got out of shooting range.

Fourth shot, I hit something. Could have been the cans. I think Dad shot his BB gun at the same time I did or stomped on the ground. Or perhaps a gust of wind blew at that moment. Something made the cans fall and Dad decided I was ready.

I was not.

We walked across the field to the railroad tracks, trying to scare up dinner. We'd sneak up quietly, once Dad got me to stop talking, and kick at the brush piles or the old fencing. Rabbits would run. Dad would shoot. I would pray.

"Lord, please don't let Dad hit any rabbits. I'd like pancakes for supper tonight."

God, my friends, hears our prayers.

He may not have healed my eyes in the manner Mom and Dad would have liked, but He didn't make me eat rabbit that night.

10

FIELD WORK

A COMBINE HOPPER full of soybeans is, well, a lot of beans. When that hopper is offloaded into the bed of a farm truck so that the bed is full, well, that's a fun place for a kid to play. And a farm truck full of beans that's driven into town and has arrived at the local mill, that's a payday waiting to happen.

That's where we were, Mom, Sis, and me. On the south side of the village of Marine at the Mill, waiting in line. We had a load of soybeans that filled the bed of our old farm truck, a well-used red Ford. Dad was proud of that truck and proud of his family; he had our names painted on the driver's side door.

Mom pulled the truck up onto the giant scale so the mill guys could weigh the load. Once they buzzed an all clear, she'd pull forward into the dumping area of the granary, where steel grates covering giant augers served as the floor.

This always made her nervous, but the mill men would direct her, and signal with their hands for her to stop once the front truck tires sat squarely on the old wooden hoist.

On this October day, Sis was sound asleep on the farm truck's bench seat. Mom and I got out and watched as the mill men lowered the tailgate, then hit the hoist to raise the front of the truck. Beans began to spill out, tumbling faster as the truck rose in the air. Sis slept soundly through it all.

That girl always has been a sound sleeper.

Now, about playing in a load of soybeans.

We had our own bin and auger at home, and Dad would store a portion of the crop there to sell at a later time. He was banking on the hope that the price of soybeans would go up, and made it a point to pass the mill to see the prices posted every time we drove into town. But for the time being, Dad would hitch a wagon full of beans to a tractor, hit the hoist, and raise the wagon's bed, just like the professionals did it in town.

Sis and I would climb up into the pile of beans, brooms in hand, and sort of sweep the beans toward the lower end of the wagon. Of course, we'd also sweep the brooms at each other. We'd ride the piles of beans as they slid down the incline, then we'd climb to the top again. Sweep, ride, climb. We'd repeat this game until the wagon was lowered, empty, and ready for another load.

On one October day, I got a bean stuck in my nose.

There it stayed, stuck solid, and causing a world of hurt. I reacted like any farm boy told he was "getting so big." I began to cry. Crying only made things swell, which made things snotty and bloody, which made everything hurt all the more.

Mom talked of taking me to the emergency room. Dad, however, pulled his pocket handkerchief out, the red bandana kind, and gently worked the bean from what felt like the bridge of my nose and back out my nostril.

I've carried a handkerchief ever since. I may not know beans about beans, but I carry one anyway. Just in case.

11

MAIL CALL

"Goin' down to get the mail!"

I don't know why we always said "down." Our 170-acre farm didn't have a "down," or an "up" for that matter. The fields, the pasture, and especially the lane out to the high-way, were flat as Mom's morning pancakes. But one of us would announce that we were "goin' down to get the mail," and we'd set off for the daily adventure.

That trip could take a few minutes by bike, a few more by tractor, or even longer if we walked it, especially if we got distracted along the way. Blackberry bushes, both tame and wild, ran along the pasture fence and may have needed picking. The horses, Rusty and Sandy, may have stuck their noses over the fence for a nuzzle, and how could we not give them a little affection? Or, if Mom was along for the mail retrieval, there may have been a few weeds to pull by the shrubs near the end of our long lane.

Those shrubs marked the place where water drained off the fields into the pasture pond. When I was really little, that run-off point was covered by a wooden bridge, which sagged even then with age. Anyone unfamiliar with the bridge got a jolt as they sped up our lane. They didn't speed on their way home, I promise.

I suppose town folks will never appreciate the adventure that "goin' down to get the mail" can be. Their mail is in a box mounted just outside the front door, or perhaps on a pole at their driveway's end. Hardly an adventure at all. But for us watching for the mailman, or in our case, our mail-woman Mrs. Stille, was a daily ritual and a source of entertainment. After all, you never knew what you might find.

Photos, for example, came in our mail. Photos that were made from the negatives we'd send in a special Kodak envelope, complete with the 67 cents in coins that it cost to develop them. I guess we didn't do this often; the family albums Mom put together go from Christmas to Easter to Halloween and back to Christmas, usually within the span of a few pages.

Or the Sears catalogue would arrive, and Mom could order a new blouse, which she typically returned. Or the spring botanical magazine, which Dad used to buy wisteria and honeysuckle bushes. Or the new *Reader's Digest*, which I read from cover to cover. That magazine became the source of my bounty of jokes, gleaned from the "Humor in Uniform" and "Life in These United States" columns.

Or the Sunday paper. On our way home from church, Dad would pull into the lane, stop, and one of us kids would hop out and retrieve the paper from our mailbox. That afternoon, Sis and I would read the comics, Dad would scan the editorials, and Mom would fix dinner. Fried chicken, or meatloaf, or a pork roast, always with mashed potatoes and corn. Mom considered corn a vegetable, and we didn't argue.

Yep, goin' down to get the mail was a big deal. It was our internet, our social media, our means to stay connected— something I wish for every family.

12

ERNA'S TURN

EMPATHY IS a fancy word I didn't use as a kid. I understood its meaning, though. When I saw my mom cry, I cried. If my dad was angry, I felt anger, too. And if my little sister vomited in the backseat of the car as we drove through the hills of Missouri, on our way to Silver Dollar City for a family vacation, well...

As I said. I understood empathy.

That's what I felt for Erna, my dad's oldest sister, who was both my aunt and my godmother. Empathy, and love.

Sympathy is what most folks felt for her. When you hear her life story, you may understand why. You may also understand why she wanted none of it. Understanding, yes. Sympathy? Well, I'll let her explain.

"I was born April 2, 1917, in Nokomis, Illinois. I was the fourth in a family that would eventually grow to ten children. My oldest brother and sister died as infants and Elmer, my older brother, was two when I came along.

"We worked from the time we were little. We were what the poor people called poor. We had nothing.

"I went to a one-room schoolhouse in Alhambra, then went to a school in Marine for a while. At ten years old, I went to my aunt's. I stayed there until I was eighteen. My parents just couldn't afford to keep me at home.

"I completed most of eighth grade, then I was taken out of public school to attend confirmation classes at a Lutheran church. Afterwards, I returned to Greenville to take the eighth-grade exam. One of the others taking the test cheated, and the papers were taken up and we were sent home. I had wanted to be a nurse or a schoolteacher, but since I didn't have an Eighth Grade Certificate, that took care of that. So, I returned to work at my aunt's house.

"I moved back in with Mom and Dad in the spring of 1935. That fall, I got a job in St. Louis and moved there, but I only stayed about a year. I was diagnosed with rheumatoid arthritis. I was in and out of the hospital for a series of surgeries and finally told to restrict my physical activity. I couldn't work, so it was back to Mom and Dad's.

"Not long after moving home, I married Erwin Smith. We lived on a rented farm for ten years, then bought a farm of our own just south of Troy. It was 1948, and life was good.

"You know that story about Lassie finding Timmy in a well? That actually happened, except I was Timmy, and it was Erwin who found me in the shaft of our farm's well. It took Erwin and a number of our neighbors many hours to dig and lift me out. Made me a local celebrity for a while. Also made my battle with arthritis much more difficult.

"We sold the farm. We used the money to buy a new home in Highland, and settled into retirement far earlier than we had planned. That was April 1965. Three months later, Erwin's heart gave out, and he passed away. He was 55.

"I was heartbroken.

"I sold our new home, moved to a smaller house in Troy, and did what I could to take care of my family and friends, while they took care of me. My nieces and nephews came to stay, and we made crafts and played in the garden. I painted a toy box for my godson. Life was good."

Erna spent the last five years of her life in nursing homes, first in Breese, then in Hitz Memorial Home in Alhambra. Sis and I attended Alhambra Elementary, and Hitz Home was just a few blocks away, so we walked over to visit Aunt Erna. She'd tell us stories and listen to us tell stories of our own, then she'd share her latest poem.

Aunt Erna was confined to her bed, lying on her back, creating poetry in her head. The lines were recited to the nurses at Hitz Home, or dictated to a tape recorder, using the pressure of her head to turn on and off a pedal switch attached to the machine.

The poems were about life on a farm, going blackberry picking, being a true friend, and having faith in God.

Her poems were published in the *Troy Times-Tribune* under the title, "The Poet's Corner." The newspaper even held annual poetry contests in her honor.

Though it certainly wasn't the way she planned it, once again life was good.

Erna passed in late November 1977. I had just turned 13. I remember attending her funeral at Friedens United Church of Christ in Troy, hearing the soprano soloist sing "In the Garden," and seeing my dad cry.

Empathy means to understand and share the feelings of another. And faith is love unseen.

I cried, too.

13

SUNDAY SCHOOL

THIRTEEN SUNDAY SCHOOL perfect attendance award pins should provide a pretty good window into my misspent youth. Pins were awarded each year on "Promotion Sunday," and Sis and I earned every one they gave.

Sunday School was held at the Marine United Church of Christ. Formerly known as the Evangelical and Reformed Church, the Marine UCC was the church my dad's parents attended; in fact, during their last years, they lived just a two-minute walk from the church. It's where the marriage of Leona (Dad's sister) to Eldon Prott took place, where the weddings of their daughters Joan (to Gene Kessinger) and Karen (to Joe Schultz) were held. It's the church where Uncle Les and Aunt Eileen were members and where their daughter Sharon married Jim Geiseking. So, of course, it was our church, too.

It was typically Mom's job to get Sis and I dressed for Sunday School, and Dad's job to drive us to Marine. That Illinois town was just a short trip by train from St. Louis, and folks at the former turn of the century would ride out of the city and take in the fresh air of Illinois countryside.

With constant visitors, the little town had more than its fair share of storefront bakeries, groceries, and taverns. Many of those were still around in the '60s, and, if we were good, Dad would stop at one of them (the bakery or the grocery, not the tavern), and let us each pick out a donut or candy bar.

Thus, the incentive for perfect attendance.

Of course, it wasn't strictly about the candy. Sunday School was learning about Jesus and singing songs like "…a Farmer and a Bug, looking down with tender love. Watch your eyes, watch your eyes, what they see."

Well, that's the way Mom remembers me singing those words. Only much later did I learn, "There's a Father up above, looking down with tender love…." Much better, though I've never minded the idea of God as a farmer.

One particular Sunday lesson wasn't about Jesus or a Farmer's love; it was Show & Tell Sunday, and I brought a cat. In a box. Yes sir, a real live cat. How I got it past Dad and into the car, I'll never know. Why it stayed in the box until it was my turn for Show & Tell, I'll never know. And how many people it took to find that cat once it flew out of the box, ran, and hid somewhere in the Sunday School wing of our church, I'll never know.

I don't think I got a donut that week.

The rule was that a kid could miss two Sundays each year and still earn the perfect attendance pin. I discovered this amazing fact and decided to try it out.

"I'm sick," I told Mom. She did that thing all moms do, pressed her hands on my fat cheeks.

"You don't feel warm," she said; "You can go to Sunday School."

But I was having none of it. "I'm sick," I repeated.

I stayed home. Sis went to Marine with Dad and came home with a candy bar, which she gladly ate in front of me.

I never played hooky again.

14

THE SOUTH BARN

THE SKY SEEMS BIGGER when you live in the country, especially when you're a little kid. It seems like you can see forever, even if the horizon stops at the trees that divide your property from the Conrad family farm, perhaps a mile to the west. And at night, the stars seem brighter, and the distance from the old house to the south barn farther than during the day.

Dad hadn't answered Mom's call for supper, so she sent me out to the south barn to get him. It was late fall and fully dark outside. I had to cross the entire backyard by myself, stopping at the pole that served as one end of Mom's laundry line. The other was an old maple tree that stood on the opposite end, far closer to the kitchen and Mom than where I was now standing.

At least the pole had a large light at its peak; a metal box with a lever allowed us to turn the light on or off as needed.

I needed it on, and I wasn't yet tall enough to reach it, but Dad had flipped the lever earlier, so I was safe.

From there, I had to walk behind the well house and over to the north entrance of the south barn. About the same size as the north barn and built at the same time, the south barn was used as a farrowing house (where sows give birth to piglets) and feed storage. It had a narrow loft where we stored extra straw bales.

Light was spilling out of the open door, but Dad wasn't at the entry. Or in the storage room. Or with the sows. He was on the floor below the loft, the wind knocked out of him. (Years later, I knocked the wind out of Mom, but that's a different story.)

I ran as fast as my little legs could take me, through the darkness, under that big, open sky. Back to the porch, and into the kitchen, to get Mom. That part of the story is clear in my mind even now. What happened next, I truly don't recall, though Mom later told me Dad was on his feet by the time we returned. He wasn't exactly fine, but good enough to come in and eat supper.

Have I mentioned that Buske translates from Polish to "neither rain nor sleet nor falls from the hayloft will keep us from eating a home-cooked meal"?

We spent a lot of hours between those three barns, carrying water from well number two to the troughs, hoisting bales of straw from the hay wagon up into the lofts, scooping corn from the toolshed crib. There were lights in every building, and a radio, wired to every entry switch. When you turned on the lights, the "Voice of St. Louis" would ring in your ears. Along with a lot of static.

Those three barns served us well.

Until the tornado came.

15

CHRISTMAS IN THE OLD HOUSE

OUR FAMILY STARTED PREPARING for Christmas each year in the same way.

Around the first of December, Mom would stop by Maedge's Store, one of a handful of private homes that doubled as general stores in Marine. She'd order a half pound of orange slices, a quarter pound of bridge mix, and a half pound of chocolate stars. No surprise, the stars were my favorite. In a few weeks, she'd pick up the order, the candy prepared for her in brown paper packages with hand-written labels.

THAT SAME WEEK, Dad would take Sis and I over to the Conrad's farm to pick out a tree. We'd walk up and down, up and down the few rows of trees trying to find the perfect one. After much discussion with Dad, we'd settle on a doozy—far too tall or far too wide or one with a few bare spots we could turn to the back. Dad would write "BUSKE" on an old bread sack and tie it to the tree, then stop by Mr. Conrad's farmhouse to give him five dollars. If Mr. Conrad wasn't home, Dad would pay him when they saw each other at church on Sunday.

DURING THE SECOND week of December, Sis and I could be overheard practicing our lines. The annual Sunday School pageant at church was always the third Sunday of the month.

"I, said the donkey, all shaggy and brown. I carried His mother up hill and down. I carried His mother to Bethlehem town. I, said the donkey, all shaggy and brown."

Those were my lines. I was too young to be a shepherd or a king. I don't remember what lines Sis had, but I know she was cast as an angel. If her Sunday school teachers only knew....

BY THE FIFTEENTH OF DECEMBER, we'd hang lights around the windows and front door on our porch.

We added a new display one Christmas, a blow mold of Santa in a sleigh with a set of flying reindeer. Unfortunately, Bouncer, our oversized mutt, chewed right through the electric cord the first night we plugged Santa in. Thanks to Bouncer, Santa didn't get lit anymore that Christmas.

Every week in December, and usually through the winter months, Mom would drag the family laundry to a laundromat in Staunton. She had to do this when the well was low and had only enough water to take care of the livestock. Staunton had a Ben Franklin store near the laundromat, which meant we could Christmas shop a little.

After a bit of Christmas shopping, Mom would take Sis and I across the street to Jubelt's Bakery for a donut. I always picked a chocolate long john, possibly because it was the biggest donut in the glass case.

With only a few days left before Christmas, the four of us would go to St. Louis to see the decorated shop windows at Famous-Barr. And, more important, to see Santa Claus, who lived on Famous' sixth floor.

One year, Sis and I got ice skates from Santa. He must have had some returns from the previous year because the skates were second hand. But, we didn't care—we just wanted to go skating.

The little pond behind our old house was pretty rough, and skating on it meant going out to the pasture (and behind the outhouse). So, Dad covered the side yard with sheets of plastic, then trimmed the large oval with a roll of corrugated tin, which created an outside edge about six inches tall. He filled our new rink with water from a hose, then let nature take its course.

Soon we were skating on our freshly frozen handmade pond. Or we tried to. We spent more time falling down and getting up than actually skating. Mom's clothesline split the rink at a diagonal above our heads, but neither Sis nor I were tall enough to reach the wire and pull ourselves up. Still, we had fun and enjoyed a very Merry Christmas!

PART II

FIVE-FOOT FORWARD

My Grandparents, Eddie and Irene Hoffmann, and me, rockin'
my church Confirmation suit. We're standing in front of the new
house, built just five feet in front of the old one.

16

MILKMEN AND HOUSE PLANS: 1974

HOWIE WAS the name of our milkman. He came to our farm once a week, driving a milk truck with the name Ruehrop's Dairy painted on its side. Howie had married one of the Ruehrop girls, becoming a husband and milkman in one fell swoop. He was a simple man, and his milk route was an example of simpler days in rural America in the 1960s.

By 1973, however, things were really beginning to change. Here's a small example: while our milk still came in glass bottles, and Howie still brought four each week, if Sis and I were especially good, Mom would ask for three quarts of whole milk and one quart of chocolate milk. That cost a bit more, and Howie would smile and take out the latest gadget: a pocket calculator.

This new toy could figure out the total price Mom owed for the order. Fascinating stuff—especially for us, not because we were getting chocolate milk, but because calculators were a great invention. Not only was addition and subtraction faster, but you could type 0.7734, turn the calculator over, and see the word, "hello."

Sis and I were easily entertained.

That same year, Dad started drawing up plans for a new house. The old house was, as the lyric goes, "still standing, though the paint was cracked and dry." It was drafty, dusty, and anything but modern. Tearing down the "cabin" portion of the house and adding a new section to the "Victorian" portion would cost as much as starting fresh, so Dad borrowed $30,000, shared his hand-drawn sketches with an architect, and employed Aviston Lumber Company to start construction on a ranch-style home.

They broke ground the following winter. That $30,000 covered everything: labor, materials, even the new furnishings. The hog market was high, which allowed Dad to make double payments on the bank loan most months. The new payment schedule was figured both by hand and by, what else, a calculator.

Labor costs were low, in part because Mom agreed to feed the entire construction crew. She fried chicken or served homemade pork roast and dumplings. She made gallons of mashed potatoes and gravy and cooked green beans she'd canned the previous summer. She baked cakes and cookies while Dad passed around cold bottles of beer he kept in the well house. Between Mom's cooking and Dad's stories, those boys were well fed and plenty full when they headed home each day.

A celebration was held when the house was finished. Everyone who worked on the house—carpenters, bricklayers, friends, and family members—came for a wonderful picnic one Saturday in May. We set out straw bales across the lawn with wood planks between them to serve as extra seating. We placed butchering tables on sawhorses in the garage and on the driveway to hold the food, and we spent the day playing horseshoes, volleyball, and softball.

In the rain. It rained all morning and part of the afternoon. Still, we celebrated.

Straw bales and wood planks became foot bridges to cross running streams of water. Folks crowded into the garage and spilled into the new basement. Cars got stuck where they'd been parked along our lane and in our pasture.

I think Mom spent a week after that shindig, cleaning up the mud.

We moved into the new house on June 3, 1974, which happened to be Sis's 8th birthday. We celebrated with cake and ice cream, sitting around our new kitchen table in our brand-new home. Then we washed it all down with, what else, a glass of freshly delivered milk, thanks to Howie.

17

PANCAKES FOR BREAKFAST

OUR FAMILY LIKED BREAKFAST—PANCAKES, bacon, waffles, more bacon, toast, and still more bacon—which meant Mom spent many mornings at the stove, flipping pancakes and frying, you guessed it: bacon.

Sizzling meat on a hot griddle can cause a bit of smoke, especially in a small 1970s kitchen with a weak stove vent (which, to be fair to the vent switch, was often neglected or forgotten entirely until it was too late). As you can imagine, very few breakfasts were served in the new house without the smoke detector sounding the alarm.

The detector in question was mounted over my sister's bedroom door, which opened directly onto the kitchen. To get the alarm to stop, Sis would get out of bed, open her door, then fan the door back and forth.

To this day, the holy trinity to me means saying grace, eating Mom's pancakes, and hearing Sis yell out, "Stop, drop, and roll!"

Once breakfast was over, we'd clear the table while Mom started the dishes and watched for the school bus from the kitchen window. She'd call out when she spotted the bus crossing the railroad tracks on State Route 4, and Sis and I would grab our books and start down the lane.

Our lane was a long walk for elementary-school kids, especially on the days when I had to carry my snare drum for band practice. Thankfully, the bus driver passed our house, used the state rest area a quarter mile down the road to turn around, then picked up the little Weber girls who lived on the farm next door, and finally returned to the end of our lane so that we could board. Still, I'd come huffing and puffing as I got to the bus.

During those few minutes after the kitchen table was cleared and before Mom spotted the bus at the railroad crossing, Dad, Sis, and I would play a hand or two of pinochle. This was the favorite card game of my Great Aunt Rosabell (Rosie) and Great Uncle Leo (Bud) Grotefendt.

Rosie and Bud taught us to play pinochle during their visits to our farm—typically every other week, often on Thursday evenings, and always unannounced. They'd show up right around the end of supper, pull up chairs, and join us around our small kitchen table.

That first kitchen set was a metal affair featuring four chairs covered in an olive-green floral pattern. I'm certain they were pretty in their 1974 showroom, and perhaps they were comfortable for slender folks. But my family is of solid German stock, and Great Uncle Bud wasn't great in name only. He pulled that chair up to the table, sat on the stylish green floral, and proceeded straight to the floor.

We played pinochle in the dining room that night. That set was made of solid wood.

18

THE BIG RED SHED

"I backed over Mom."

More words came tumbling out, but those were the words Dad heard me say, and they were enough. He jumped on the tractor I'd driven out to the south 40—the acreage on the far side of the railroad tracks—took the wheel from my hands, and steered us back toward the house, the big red shed, and Mom.

I should back up. Not over Mom again, but to the beginning of the story.

Dad was on the combine harvesting beans or corn, I don't remember which, that fall day. The field he was working lay on the south end of our farm, a tract of land divided by a railroad track that carried coal from Coffeen, Illinois, to East St. Louis. When I was really young, trains always had a caboose, and I'd wave at the man in the caboose, he'd wave back, and all would be right with the world.

But on this day, all was definitely not right, because Mom was lying on the floor of the big red shed. She could wave, but she couldn't catch her breath. All she said was, "Go get your dad."

Ach, I'm ahead of myself again.

So, Dad was out in the field, and I was supposed to bring a farm wagon out to him. I had to slide open the large metal doors of the big red shed, start the tractor, and hook it up to the wagon. And yes, most farmers would call it a machine shed, and some county folks might call it a pole shed, but we called it the big red shed.

It was built after a tornado hit our farm in 1975. That storm blew down both of the smaller machine sheds that stood on the south edge of the homestead. It also blew off part of the south barn, knocked two large barrels of gasoline and diesel fuel off their stands, and blew a rock through the picture window of our new house. After all that damage was cleaned up, we built the big red shed, where we housed the combine, tractors, planter, plows, and all of the assorted equipment to run a small farm.

Hmmm, now where was I?

Oh. So Mom followed me out to the big red shed and stood beside the farm wagon, ready to drop a pin in the hitch so that I could pull it out to the field where Dad was combining beans or picking corn. Are you with me? And I, being eleven years old and just tall enough to reach the clutch, had backed the tractor to the wagon but not quite far enough for her to put in the pin.

A little farther. And boom! Mom was on the ground, lying partially under the farm wagon, the wind knocked out of her. That's when she'd said, "Go get your dad."

I went to get Dad, as fast as that old tractor could go. I drove down our lane, turned right onto Illinois Highway 4, then headed up the hill toward the railroad track crossing at fourteen miles an hour. I used my left arm to wave at the traffic building behind me, letting them know it was okay to pass. I used my right hand to steer the tractor—the promised wagon not hitched behind me but back in the big red shed, with Mom underneath it. And I wondered what the heck I would say to Dad.

"I backed over Mom."

Thankfully, by the time he and I returned, Sis was standing beside Mom, who was now also standing, having caught her breath. Everyone was okay. After a bit, everything went back to normal. Dad hooked up the wagon and returned to the field. Mom went up to the porch to sit for a while, then forgave me for running over her.

At least I think she did.

From that day forward, she drove the tractor, and I put in the pin.

19

SHOWER STALLS

WE THOUGHT WE WERE RICH.

Our new home had not one, but two bathrooms—and both had running water. Both also had sinks with large vanities and working toilets. The "front" bathroom had a tub, while the "back" bathroom had a round shower. Literally, the shower stall was round, with a curved fiberglass door to complete the circle.

And that's where we all cleaned up. Not the front bathroom; that was for guests. The four of us shared the back bathroom, which was only accessible by walking through my parent's bedroom.

School mornings went something like this:

Mom would put on a housecoat, slip out of the bedroom, and start breakfast. Dad would stay in bed just a little longer, listening to KMOX on the radio. I'd take some clothes from my dresser, leave my bedroom, walk through my parents' bedroom to the back bathroom, shower, dress, and trade places with Sis. She'd be waiting outside the bathroom door, wearing her pajamas and holding a change of clothing, ready to take her turn.

Follow all of that?

This routine went on for years—through adolescence, the junior high and high school years, even through college and my first years of teaching.

Not awkward. Not awkward at all.

I learned to shave in that bathroom mirror. I learned that Old Spice wasn't just for old men. I learned that the rest of the world had hot-water faucets on the left, cold on the right. The plumbers installed ours in reverse, which was an early-morning wake-up call if you forgot.

Summer mornings didn't require the same routine. No school meant we were free to play, feed the livestock, and work in the fields. That meant a shower before bedtime, to wash off the day's work.

But summers also meant less water in the well. So Dad hauled water from Hamel using a metal tank he loaded onto the truck. A metal tank that leaked, so that, as he drove back from Hamel, a trickle of water left a trail down Highway 4. The tank was emptied by hose into the well, and we used the fresh water sparingly so that it lasted until the next week's load.

During a drought, evening showers were timed. The timer was Mom, who stood outside the bathroom door and yelled, "That's enough water!"

In three minutes or less, we "cleaned up."

20

SON OF A LIFE-INSURANCE SALESMAN

THERE WAS a time in his life when Dad farmed 170 acres and raised 100 head of hogs annually. A time when he drove an oil spreader across southern Illinois for a company based in Collinsville. A time when he clerked sales for auctioneers throughout Madison and Bond counties.

All of that would be enough to keep any man busy six days a week—driving a truck during the day, feeding animals in the evenings, planting crops on weekends, clerking auctions on the occasional Saturday. But somehow, Dad also found time to sell life insurance for the Woodmen of the World company. He squeezed it in on Friday evenings, after the hogs were fed.

I didn't see him until I was eleven years old—or so I said to him, when I was in my forties and he in his seventies. I was teasing him, but we both knew it was true. It's just what guys do, work hard to provide for their family.

Dad stopped working as an insurance salesman after just a few years, though he stayed active with the Woodmen of the World fraternity for the rest of his life. He and his buddies were always doing something: hosting a dance, selling raffle tickets, organizing a picnic, building a float.

They built a float for the annual Highland Homecoming parade only once. They used a farm hay wagon, framed the sides with chicken wire stretched over two by fours, and stuffed the holes in the chicken wire with artificial flowers made of green and white tissue. Really. I can't make this stuff up.

The parade was held on Friday night and a bunch of their kids, including me, got to ride on the bed of this tissue-covered wagon. I suppose we tossed out candy along the parade route; I was pretty young, and I don't remember.

Dad didn't remember, either—that I had ridden the float, I mean. Because, at the end of the route, as his buddies backed the wagon into a shed to await the next evening's festivities, Dad left. Without me.

He walked back with Uncle Les to the town square, with its amusement rides and concession stands. It was Aunt Eileen and my Mom who realized I was missing, and they had me paged over the loudspeakers while they retraced Dad's steps to the shed. They found me patiently playing with the tissue flowers.

We all met up with Dad and Uncle Les at the concession stand that sold beer. I don't know how many weeks passed before Mom forgave him.

Dad stuck with the auctioneers for most of his life as well. Long after the parade mess, Dad took me along on sale days, allowing me to run tickets between the auctioneer's truck and the shed where the auctioneer's wife served as cashier. I earned five dollars a day.

Dad and I would begin the day in his pick-up, listening to KMOX radio and the Saturday morning comedy hour. Sometimes we'd talk about what was happening on the farm, or school, or just listen to Bob Hardy tell long-winded jokes on the air.

One Saturday, when I was in seventh grade, Dad started the truck and started our conversation with a question. "Your Mom says you had a sex education unit at school."

"Yep," I said.

"Any questions?" he asked.

"Nope," I replied.

And we went back to the comedy hour.

21

SWIMMING LESSONS

ONE OF THE perks of life in the new house was an air conditioner, which promised cool air all summer long. That is, when Mom turned it on.

Mom had rules about the air conditioning.

Rule #1: It was a sin to run the air conditioner before June 1.

Rule #2: It was another sin to do the same after August 31. Such pleasantries as cool air were an extravagance to be enjoyed only during summer months, and even then, only in the evenings.

Mom would turn the thermostat to "on" after supper dishes were washed and let the house cool down until bedtime— which, by the way, was set at 9 o'clock and remained so throughout her lifetime. Then, at about 10 o'clock, I'd hear

Mom get out of bed, gently step into the hall, and firmly turn the thermostat to "off." No need to pay for forced, cool air once we were all asleep.

Not that any of us was sleeping.

Well, Dad was sleeping. He could sleep no matter the temperature, and he snored like a chainsaw. Dad could be heard from one end of our new, open floor plan to the other, even with the bedroom doors closed.

On the other hand, Mom could never sleep, and had a habit of getting up around midnight and going to the kitchen to eat a few saltine crackers to settle her stomach. Then she'd check on Janet and me, to make sure we were snug in our beds, by poking her head into our rooms and turning on the overhead light. Seeing us under the covers, she'd then turn the light off, leaving us to go back to sleep—or, more likely, to finally fall asleep now that her evening ritual was complete.

We spent long hot summer days riding our bikes around the block, which, in the country, could be a distance of three to five miles, depending on which "block" we chose. Or we worked in the garden, played on the swing set, or swam in our farm pond, a man-made watering hole the cows, sheep, and horses also used to cool down and, uh, go about their business.

Once, Mom and Dad took us to a real live pool party, held at a real live in-ground neighborhood pool. Mom helped the ladies set up the buffet line. Dad grabbed a beer and talked with his buddies. Sis was still in diapers and stayed on the sidelines. I went directly to the pool.

I remember being in water over my head, waving my hands above the water line, hoping someone would rescue me. Someone did, though I don't remember who or what happened next.

I lived, but it wouldn't be the last time I'd feel like I was "in over my head."

A few summers later, Mom signed Sis and me up for swimming lessons. These annual camps were held at the Highland City Pool, built in the very park where Mom had grown up and where Grandma had sold snow cones to countless kids looking for a way to cool down in the summer heat.

It's also where, each and every year, I had the opportunity to fail the swimming class.

I could "bob" and open my eyes under the water, but heck, I struggled to see anything above the water with my glasses on, so I certainly wasn't identifying anything under the water without them.

I could relax and breathe deeply like the teacher asked me, but I never got the hang of floating on my back. That seemed to be a prerequisite for moving on. While the other kids graduated to the deep end, I stayed in the shallows, bobbing and weaving around kids younger than me. I tried to stay cool—literally and figuratively.

At least the kids in the pool were better company than the cows in the pond.

22

BASEBALL, HOTDOGS, APPLE PIE, & 4-H

"What am I doing here?" I asked myself. I was thinking I should be out in right field. I liked right field. No one ever hits a ball to the guy in right field. Well, maybe in professional baseball, but not in a 4-H softball league. Hardly ever, anyway.

Yet there I was, playing second base at Township Park, just across the field from our elementary school. My team, Alhambra Silver Creek, was battling the guys from Marine's 4-H Club. The game was under the lights and we were under pressure to win—or at least, not to embarrass ourselves. Again.

Truth was, we won as many games as we lost. It's just that, we were *that* group of kids—not exceptionally athletic, not exceptionally talented. Just a group of nice guys and gals who met in the basement of Alhambra Township's Meeting

Hall, learning Robert's Rules of Order as we held our monthly 4-H meetings.

Every meeting began with the Pledge.

"I pledge my HEAD to clearer thinking, my HEART to greater loyalty, my HANDS to larger service, and my HEALTH to better living, for my club, my community, my country, and my world."

Old business was read by the secretary who was elected based on niceness, not on public oration skills.

New business focused on what projects we'd selected to show at the Madison County Fair. It was always held during the hottest part of July each year on the Lindendale Park grounds in the city of Highland.

Some of the kids showed hogs, or cattle, or sheep. A few others, rabbits or chickens. Most of us took on gardening or leather-making. I got a blue ribbon on a photography project one year and a red ribbon on a leather belt I hand tooled and stained. Sis often took blue ribbons in baking. I especially liked her summer fruit pizza, because it had a cream cheese base and…

Getting back to the ballgame.

Todd Maedge was at the plate, batting for Marine. Todd was incredibly athletic and talented. He was also the son of one of Dad's drinking buddies, Marvin. Todd and I got along alright, but let's just say that there was a friendly rivalry between us. There he stood at the plate, batting for Marine, and I was covering second base.

"…my HEAD to clearer thinking…"

All I thought was, "Please God, let Todd strike out." Was that so wrong?

"…my HEART to greater loyalty…"

I was loyal to my teammates—Jim Kaegel, David Stille, the Reichmann boys. They were all great guys, and better ball players than I.

And I was loyal to my dad, who had pitched for his softball team when he was a kid in 4-H, and typically pitched when the guys got together at Deck's Prairie on the old Schrumpf farm. Dad always carried a burlap sack of wooden baseball bats, gloves, and softballs in the trunk of the car. Always. He was in the stands on this night, shouting and cheering my team on, trying to yell louder than Marvin.

"…my HANDS to larger service…"

My right hand was shaking in the red Rawlings glove. My left hand was shaking, and it had no place to hide. And neither hand would qualify as large.

THWACK! Todd hit a line drive. Hard. Straight into my outstretched glove. *MY* glove.

I was dazed. I was dazzled. After the initial shock, I remembered to touch second base, then remove the ball from my glove and throw it to the guy covering third. Todd was out. The guy sliding into second was out, but the guy running to third was safe.

Didn't matter.

I'd caught the ball. And Dad had seen me do it.

I'd caught the ball, mostly thanks to luck.

And I caught it *"...for my club, my community, my country, and my world."*

But mostly, for my dad.

23

DISHPAN HANDS

THE KITCHEN SINK in our new house was centered on a window that faced south. It was a double sink, and Mom would place a plastic tub in the right-hand side, then fill it with hot water and plenty of dish soap. She used the makeshift liner so that she could carry the used dishwater out the back door and toss it over the pasture fence. Less grease and grime coated the pipes that way.

My sister and I stood on the left side, taking turns drying the supper dishes. Supper was our evening meal, and it was served at 4:30, which, during the winter, was just before sunset. We'd finish the task, hang the towels over the backs of the kitchen chairs, and start our homework.

During the summer months, however, there would still be a few hours of daylight left. The sun would shine from its southwest angle as we dried and put away the dishes.

That's when Mom would spot it. A speck. A smudge. A soap bubble that wouldn't remain where it had landed.

On her kitchen window.

"When you're finished," she'd say, "go outside and wipe the window. I'll get the inside. We need to clean off that dust." Or those streaks. Or, if Dad was taking his once-in-a-blue moon turn, we needed to "clean up the slop your father has created all the way up the window."

Now, I've been short since birth, and reaching the kitchen window required climbing up on a step stool, which we didn't have, or an old wooden ladder, which we did have. It was stored in a corner of the garage, so out I'd go to get the ladder, then back in to get the bottle of water mixed with white vinegar (Windex was for town kids) and an old cloth. I'd set the ladder at the window's base, then climb up, spray, and wipe the window clean.

Almost clean.

"Get the corners. You missed the corners."

Mom's instruction was clear, even though her voice, from inside the house, was muffled slightly by the glass.

Spritz. Rub. Smile.

"There's a big streak right in the middle."

Squirt. Polish. Wave.

"Better. Can you please wipe up and down instead of side to side?"

Mist. Pat. Squint.

"Good enough, thank you. It's getting dark. Now get your butt inside."

Looking back, I'd say Mom taught me a great lesson, one that goes something like this:

Check your view. What you see may not be what others see. Take a look from their side, and you might notice a smudge you hadn't seen before.

24

IF THE HORSESHOE FITS

You toss a Frisbee. You cast a rod. You might lob a volleyball, hurl a javelin, or fling a golf club in utter frustration. But, when playing horseshoes, you *pitch*.

Dad pitched for Grantfork Bowl, which was Grantfork's triple threat: a bowling alley, an arcade (two pinball machines and one pool table), and a watering hole—the water in this case being beer.

Mom and Dad bowled on leagues at Grantfork when I was very little. Mom would dress me in a white T-shirt and overalls. Then Dad's brother, Les, would give me a Hershey bar, just to see how much of a mess I could make. In those days, Uncle Les started phone conversations with, "You're looking good," which gives you a pretty clear picture of his sense of humor.

By the time Sis and I were a little older, Chester Hartlieb's Grantfork Bowl added a horseshoe-pitching team to its entertainment venue. Every Thursday night during the summer, the team competed as part of a league.

Dad was on the team, as was Uncle Eldon Prott. Both men were good, and practiced on Sundays at each other's farms. Uncle Les pitched, too, and so did a pipe-smoker named Wally Schrumpf.

I'll get back to Wally later.

Now, if the guys were playing in Grantfork, then Mom brought Sis and me, and we'd sit on a blanket and watch. When we got a little older, we'd go inside and play pinball or watch the older kids bowl. One of the machines featured Roy Clark of "Hee-Haw" fame. I lost a lot of quarters on that pinball machine.

If the league schedule called for play in Highland, Mom, Sis, and I didn't go. The taverns that sponsored those teams didn't cater to spectators, and there wasn't much for kids to do.

If the league schedule called for play in Pierron, well there wasn't much to do at the park in that tiny Illinois village either. Until, of course…THE SLIDE!

Once used as a fire escape at the old schoolhouse, the slide was a two-story thrill ride erected along the playground, a steel staircase with enormous piers anchoring it to the ground below.

You had to be brave. You had to be fearless. You had to be plumb stupid to think no one would get hurt and sue the village but hey, this was the early '70s, and folks didn't think about things like that.

I was brave. I was fearless. I let Sis go first, because I was also a gentleman.

She survived, so I took my turn, and we both spent the evening free falling on this new wonder, watching Dad and Uncle Eldon win another round of horseshoes, and running back to Mom, who sat near the blanket, for snacks. This was kid heaven!

Once it was well past dark, Mom pulled us away from the fun and drove us home. The team had another round or two to play, so Dad and Eldon and Wally stayed behind.

You remember Wally?

Wally, officially Wallace P. Schrumpf, was known to his friends as "Governor." He and his wife, Shirley, were a generation older than my folks, but they had become life-long friends.

Before we kids came along, and before the farm's lane was paved, the Governor and Shirley would spend a Saturday evening playing euchre with Mom and Dad. If it had rained recently, they'd park at the edge of the lane, Dad would drive the tractor down, and they'd ride up to the house together. Wally would sit on Dad's right, his pipe and tobacco close at hand.

On this fateful evening, well after dark and just after the final match on the horseshoe pits, Wally decided he wanted to take a turn on THE SLIDE. Off they went, Dad and Wally, climbing up the steel stairs, none too steady on their feet, thanks to a long evening of pitching and drinking.

Dad went down first, letting gravity do its thing, and no doubt laughing all the way down. Wally went next. He put his pipe in his pocket, lowered his five-foot-seven-inch Swiss-German frame into the chute, and let loose.

The paramedics later said his left arm was only slightly broken. His pipe and tobacco survived. Thank goodness he pitched with his right hand.

Slide on home, folks, and take your turn every chance you can.

25

COMPANY COMING

Dad sat in the orange-checked La-Z-Boy recliner. Sis and I took turns, sprawled either on the sofa or the floor. Mom joined us after the supper dishes were done. She never did anything until the dishes were put away and the kitchen was "cleaned up."

If it were summer, Sis and I were most likely in T-shirts and shorts, not yet changed for bed. Mom may have already changed into her nightgown and a housecoat.

Dad was in his underwear.

If it were winter, Sis, Mom, and I were each under our own afghans, hand made by Mom's Aunt Rose. Under the afghan, Mom wore a thick cotton housecoat over her nightgown. Dad often said that Hoffmann women wore more to bed than most women wore all day.

Dad was in his underwear.

Another Saturday night on the farm, watching "All in the Family," "The Mary Tyler Moore Show," and "Hee Haw."

Until headlights were seen coming down our lane.

From his vantage point on the La-Z-Boy, Dad could see them coming first. "Them" was typically Aunt Arlene and Uncle John and their five kids: Keith, Kevin, Kent, Kurt, and Kay, or Uncle Eldon and Aunt Leona, or maybe Aunt Norma and Uncle Gerp. "Them" was never Mom's side of the family; while we saw the Hoffmann's often, it was more typically on holidays, and rarely unannounced.

After a warning shout from Dad, Mom would be up first, quickly change back into her daytime clothes, then pull things from the chest freezer in the basement. She learned early on to keep a cake, or cookies, or a loaf of zucchini bread on hand, just in case someone dropped in.

Dad would be up next, looking out the window to identify the vehicle so that he knew who was coming down the lane. Then he'd run back to the bedroom to, well, put clothes on.

Sis and I were told to go outside and greet our guests—and to stall, at least for a minute or two.

To be fair, Dad's brothers and sisters came "home" most Sundays for dinner, to the very farm we now lived on, when Dad's folks were still alive. Grandma Buske fixed a big Sunday dinner during those years, and those who could make it drove out to the family farm and ate, then stayed for the afternoon to visit.

Large family gatherings were the norm for the eight Buske kids and their spouses, and while Grandma and Grandpa Buske were gone, as was the old house, a Saturday night surprise visit from one of the Buske siblings and their family wasn't a surprise at all. And if a Saturday night went by when one of the siblings didn't stop in, we most likely showed up at their farms Sunday afternoon.

I am forever thankful for lots and lots of cousins and long afternoons or evenings, spent either outside playing softball or volleyball or a made-up game, or in the basements of each other's homes, laying out track for trains or playing ping-pong or shooting pool.

A pool game in our basement required "house rules"— meaning the house itself was in charge. The pool table, a three-quarter-sized item Dad bought at a public auction, was situated between the basement stairs and the water heater. The players had plenty of room to line up the perfect shot on either end of the table, but shots performed on either side required some fancy shooting, with pool sticks, arms, and legs held at interesting angles. The plastic Falstaff beer sign that hung above the table, with its single forty-watt bulb, didn't help matters.

Ping-pong and trains were our entertainments of choice.

After a while, Mom would call down for us kids to clean up. We'd put all the toys away and head upstairs, where she and Aunt Arlene (or Aunt Leona or Aunt Norma) would have the table set with sliced ham or summer sausage and cheese; a loaf of bread; pickles or tomatoes or whatever was in season; and the aforementioned cake or cookies. The adults would drink coffee and the talk would turn to how Uncle Les's summer sausage recipe was different from Uncle John's. Soon we'd say goodnight, and off they'd go.

Sis and I straightened up the living room, then went to bed. Dad sat in the La-Z-Boy for a few minutes, then turned in as well.

Mom did the dishes. One should never go to bed until the dishes are done.

26

RIDING THROUGH HISTORY

FINALLY, freedom! I was given four wheels and the ability to go anywhere I wanted—in the living room. I was driving my very first pedal car, painted to resemble a fire engine. It even had its own bell!

I was three.

When I turned thirteen, I was given a new form of freedom: a three-speed bicycle. There were no bells or whistles, but it did have a horn, the kind with the rubber ball you squeeze to let folks know you're coming. Since I tended to sing as I rode, I really didn't need the horn.

I rode that bike up and down the lane, out to the fields, and around the block. The "block," in this case, ran from our farm to Kaufmann Station, then down Marine Road to Fruit Road, wound back past what was once a one-room schoolhouse, then back home again. About three miles round trip. It was a good forty-minute ride. Faster, if the Robertson's dogs chased me.

The following spring, I was challenged to ride much farther. Kem and Cathy Conrad taught my Confirmation Sunday School class. They hatched a plan to host our group at their new home in the country, a sort of class picnic. Each of the Confirmands was asked to bring a bicycle to church, then, after the 10:10 service, ride out from Marine to their place.

Our farm shared a border with the Conrad's, I would ride my three-speed from church to their house and then, after the picnic, ride the last quarter mile to my own. About six miles—twice as far as my typical 'round the block.'

I thought this was a great idea. Dad thought this was a great idea. Mom thought it was an awful idea, but a vote was taken and majority ruled.

We set off that Sunday afternoon as a pack, riding together around Marine's town square, then crossing the Illinois Central Railroad tracks as we headed north out of town.

It's said that Marine got its name from a group of retired sea captains who settled the area in the early 1800s. The village wasn't incorporated until the 1860s, a full hundred years before my church friends and I came along. All we knew then was that the road ahead was mostly flat prairie, now farmland, with an occasional oil rig still pumping away on either side of us.

Jim Blumberg and I rode ahead, and quickly the pack spread out, riding two by two, with Kem and Cathy bringing up the rear. A Victorian brick mansion, topped by a widow's walk, loomed on our left. Perhaps it was the family home of one of those sea captains. I know Dad talked about playing there as a kid; he and cousin Larry hid in the secret passages behind the walls. Dad said slaves hid there during the Civil War. Possible, I suppose. Then again, Dad liked to pull my leg.

We turned onto Fruit Road, still in the lead, and soon passed the old Nike missile base. The base was part of an anti-aircraft installation, one of four placed by the U.S. government in 1954 to protect the fair city of St. Louis. No missiles were ever launched, though I understand at least one was loaded during the Cuban Missile Crisis in '62. Still, before my time.

On we pedaled. Past Bill and Esther Weber's farm. Mrs. Weber played piano for us in Sunday School. Over Illinois Route 4. Our farm was just a mile down the highway, but we were told to stick to the back roads. Past a two-story brick block I suspected was once a coach stop for travelers. An identical old home stood beside the horseshoe pits and tavern in Grantfork, where Dad threw a lot of shoes and drank a few beers. He agreed that, yes, the abandoned building might once have been a hotel. Then again…he might have been pulling my leg.

Finally, we arrived at the Conrad's new modified A-frame home, a grand example of late '70s architecture. Soon the others would join us—winded, sore, and hungry.

I'm sure we ate well and had a grand time. I guess everyone's folks came to take them—and their bicycles—home. Those details aren't as clear.

What is clear are the feelings I had as a result of this trip: a bit more grown-up, a little more independent. I'd ridden past history and written a part of my own.

27

THE MIGHTY MARINE UCC YOUTH FELLOWSHIP

ONE OF MY best friends in middle school was a Lutheran. Many of my cousins were Catholics. I'd heard of Baptists and Methodists, but didn't personally know any of them. I guess they all attended church in some other small town.

In our town, I was an "ucc" (like yuck without the 'y') a UCC kid, a member of the United Church of Christ. Saying that I was an "ucc" typically got a chuckle from folks, and it gave me the opportunity to share my faith.

There were quite a number of us teens who attended Marine UCC. We'd met each other in Sunday School, or Vacation Bible School, or in Confirmation classes. We all got along and now that we were in high school, we took the next step in church activity: the youth fellowship.

Our little chapter met on Sunday nights. Meetings included a devotional led by Reverend Griebel, a retired teacher-turned-pastor of our small-town church. We also had a game or activity often organized by yours truly. Refreshments were served at the end of the meeting, typically provided by Mrs. Griebel, a full-time pastor's wife and part-time substitute public school teacher.

We were an active group of kids. Together, we sponsored a child through an overseas Christian agency. We made the unleavened bread for communion, in part because none of us liked the traditional wafers the congregation was in the habit of using. We went ice skating and roller skating and earned money through crazy fundraising ideas—like hosting a haunted house in the basement of the church or selling hand-painted pumpkins at the main crossroads of town, or taking orders for hand-dyed Easter eggs. We paved our way and let the adult church know we wanted to be a part of their community.

Of course, we inherited some tasks from the youth groups that had gone before us. For example, we were responsible for assembling and decorating the twelve-foot Christmas tree that stood in the sanctuary. In other words, each year a bunch of kids—including my sister and me—went up the bell tower stairs to the second floor, crossed the old choir loft, then struggled into a cramped storage closet. There, we gathered and gently carried boxes and boxes of lights and ornaments down those same stairs and into the sanctuary.

Next, a few kids climbed the stairs once again, then grabbed armfuls of fake tree limbs from the storage closet and tossed them over the balcony of the choir loft down to those of us standing in the sanctuary. That is, those who were brave enough to try and catch them.

The Rev. and Mrs. Griebel watched closely. And tried not to wince.

As you can imagine, that tree had it pretty rough and was looking pretty ragged one particular Christmas. So we kids determined to raise funds for a new tree and, while we were at it, all new decorations. We were accustomed to creating unconventional fundraisers and managed to talk two farmers into letting us walk their corn fields—after those fields were harvested—and pick up stray ears of corn, which we could sell to the local grain elevator.

The first farmer who agreed was my dad, and so the first farm field we walked was our own. Dad hitched a wagon, drove the tractor out to the south forty, and gave us each a five-gallon bucket to fill. He gave a bucket to Reverend Griebel as well. His wife stayed at the house with Mom and helped prepare chili for our lunch. And so we worked side by side—a pastor, a father, and a flock of children—filling our buckets with corn. We gathered enough to fill the wagon. Well, almost.

Uncle Eldon Prott's farm was next. His kids (my cousins) had long outgrown the youth group, but he and Aunt Leona were fellow UCC folks, and they were glad to help out. Pickings were slim, but we found enough to (almost) fill another wagon. And we raised enough money to buy the church a new tree and new decorations to boot.

The Old Testament book of Leviticus would call us "the poor and the sojourners," gleaning the leftover crops. We just called ourselves kids. And Christians.

28

BACON IN THE BATHTUB

THE LITTLE COLEMAN stove went everywhere with us. So did the big red cooler with the white lid, though Mom always called it an "ice chest," not a cooler.

Mom filled that big red ice chest with packages of hamburger and bacon, homemade potato salad, and some tomatoes from the garden. Dad tossed in a few sodas and a couple of Stag beers. The cooler sat center stage in the trunk of our car, the Coleman camp stove tucked into a far corner, our four small suitcases wedged in around them.

A grocery bag of potato chips, miniature packs of boxed cereal, and Little Debbie oatmeal pies, plus paper plates and napkins, sat on top of the cooler. An old plastic table-cloth covered the lot, if we remembered to take it out of the trunk in the first place. If we forgot, it covered the spare tire until we got where we were going.

Where we were going was often anyone's guess.

Dad would turn out of our lane onto Illinois Highway 4, and about a mile later, Mom would wonder aloud if she'd turned off the stove, or the iron, or the air conditioner. Dad would just keep driving, and start singing to us—usually an old song by Gene Autry or Jim Reeves. Sis and I would ask where we were going and if the hotel would have a swimming pool. We never got an answer.

About 11:30 a.m., Dad would start looking for a roadside rest area or a "scenic overlook" with a picnic table. He was especially happy if a historic marker with a story about a Civil War battle or a description of the Trail of Tears was close by. Dad never met a monument he didn't pull off the highway to read.

Once a spot was found, the big red ice chest with the white lid was removed from the trunk. Hamburgers would soon be sizzling in a cast-iron pan, heated by the little Coleman stove. Tomatoes were sliced, and paper plates and a tablecloth laid in place. One beer and three no-name cola cans were popped. Dinner was served.

Dad would pull back on the road once our picnic had been cleaned up, the stove had cooled down, and the bright yellow Frisbee had been tossed back and forth between us, then returned to the trunk with the rest of our traveling gear. Sis and I would ask about a swimming pool again, and we'd get an answer to our plea in the form of "I Never

See Maggie Alone" or "Ol' Shep" or another of Dad's favorite tunes.

There weren't many motels to choose from, no matter where we landed that evening. Despite this, our routine was the same. Sis and I watched for vacancy signs, Dad would stop, ask at the front desk what a room cost, confer with Mom through the open window of the car, and get a "no" nod from her. This would continue until she nodded "yes" to a place deemed affordable.

Then the unpacking began. Mom and Sis would share one bed, while Dad and I slept on the other. "Slept" is a relative term, of course, as the only person who would sleep was Dad; his ability to snore kept us, and sometimes the folks staying in neighboring rooms, awake all night.

Which brings me to breakfast, and the title of this tale.

I don't remember if it was raining on that particular weekend family vacation, or if there were no picnic benches nearby. Maybe it was just because there was still food in the big red cooler, packed in fresh ice from the motel machine the night before. For whatever reason, Dad decided to set the little camping stove up so that he could fry bacon for breakfast—in the bathroom tub.

Grease splattered everywhere, creating quite the mess. After a breakfast of cereal and hot bacon sandwiches, Mom spent the rest of the morning taking Dad's name in vain. She didn't cuss, but she said "Vernon" often and with enough inflection to get her point across.

She also made sure that bathtub was cleaner than when we checked in.

Thanks to these weekend vacations, we saw an Indian burial ground, Lincoln's tomb, and the Garden of the Gods in Shawnee National Forest. The smell of bacon still triggers those travel memories, and I can hear Dad's voice as he sang to us on the way back to the farm.

It was always about the journey, not the destination.

29

EDDIE'S TURN

EVERY FAMILY HAS A STORY—PASSED down from one generation to the next, with events that have been exaggerated and facts blurred in the retelling.

You know the one. It's typically told once or twice a year, often near the end of a family gathering, when the younger kids have left the table and the older folks start saying things like, "Remember when…." About then, someone recounts the story of Great-Great Aunt so-and-so's immigration to the United States. Then one of the uncles recounts the year he caught "the big one" up at the family cabin. No fish has ever grown bigger.

This is ours. I've heard our story many times—from my grandfather, though I was too young to appreciate it; from my uncle, the family historian; and from my godmother, who filled in some of the gaps. It's the story of my great grandfather's passing and the events that helped shape our family tree.

My great grandfather's name was Edward. He was born in August 1887, and died in August 1908, most likely from a ruptured appendix. Nothing remarkable about that, until you consider Edward was only 21 years old and newly married to Josephine, my great grandmother.

Now to be clear, Edward L. Hoffmann died August 8, 1908, and his son, Edward R. Hoffmann, was born March 21, 1909, meaning Josephine was most likely unaware that she was pregnant when her husband suddenly passed away.

Imagine her pain, grief, and then surprise at learning she would be a mother—a single mother—in 1909.

In March 1909, Teddy Roosevelt had just passed the presidential baton to William Howard Taft. Henry Ford's latest contraption, the Model T, had been on the road for just six months. And Edward Robert Hoffmann, my grandpa, came into the world.

According to the story, Edward R. ("Eddie") spent most of his early years with Josephine's mother-in-law, Louisa Bollmann Hoffmann. In February 1915, Josephine married William Metzger, and together they had five children: Rose, William, Oliver, Cleda, and Isabelle. Eddie is now the eldest of six kids in what I imagine was a busy and happy household.

And that seems a fitting ending to a pretty unremarkable story. But the story doesn't end there.

Eddie was just twenty-one and in the driver's seat. His mother sat beside him, and the girls sat in the back. At least Rose was there; that's one of the pieces she filled in for me years later. Probably Cleda was as well, and maybe baby Isabelle. It was 1930, and Eddie was most likely driving one of those old Model T's, or a used Hudson, or whatever the large family could afford.

There was an accident, one that Rose said was not her brother's fault. Nonetheless, their mother, Josephine Vaupel Hoffmann Metzger, died in the hospital from complications caused by the car crash.

I know a lot about my grandfather, how he and my grandma raised six kids during the Great Depression. I know that he worked as a bus driver, a gas station manager, a night watchman, even the town Santa, to earn a living.

I've heard about his years as caretaker of the Madison County Fairgrounds and how he started the Wednesday night "blue jean" dances in the little city of Highland.

I know he lost his half-brother William, who died while fighting in North Africa during World War I. And I know he lost his son, Richard, to the war in Vietnam.

I still associate the smell of popcorn with Grandpa, having spent many years playing behind his concession stands until I was old enough to work in them myself.

But I can't imagine what it was like, growing up during a time so many of us consider "those simpler days."

My Grandpa passed on Christmas Eve 1980. He was made of sterner stuff than I. And his story is remarkable, after all.

30

THE BASEMENT

WE NEVER FINISHED THE BASEMENT.

Oh, we painted the concrete walls white, rolled out a few area rugs, and hung strands of old Christmas bulbs along the joists in the ceiling. They stayed there year-round.

The basement is where Dad kept his collection of wine, both the store-bought kind and his homemade versions. It's where Mom stored our canned tomatoes, and peaches, and pickles. It's also where Sis beat me at ping-pong, or I beat her, depending on who reported the score afterward.

Ping-pong balls still decorated the ceiling when we left the farm, forty years later.

The basement is where many of our family gatherings were held—including Thanksgiving, when the pool table became a banquet table, surrounded by folding chairs. As well as

Christmas with all of the Hoffmanns—Mom's side of the family—exchanging white-elephant gifts.

The rules to the white-elephant game changed annually. One year, everyone sat in a circle, pulling slips of paper from a bag, then followed their printed directions. "Pass your gift two people to the right." "Trade your present with your favorite relative." "Kiss the person on your left." Dad was surprised to read that one, especially since Uncle Danny was immediately to his left. But Dad, being Dad, followed directions.

It was in the basement where we held Grandma and Grandpa Hoffmann's surprise 45th wedding anniversary party, an event that filled the place with Hoffmanns, Baers, and Metzgers. Great Aunt Millie walked around with an old Kodak at her waist; she never aimed, just shot from the hip. We were amazed that so many of her pictures turned out okay, complete with the heads of her subjects.

Mom decorated the cake for that 45th anniversary party. During those years, she was always piping roses and shell edges for weddings, using star tips to create wool on Easter lambs, and icing bowl-shaped cakes into fancy doll dresses for birthdays. She completed many of those cakes in the basement kitchen. It was cooler down there, and quieter, too. That suited Mom just fine.

The basement kitchen area also had a laundry. We moved a wringer washing machine over from the cellar of the old house into the basement of the new one. Buskes don't replace what isn't broken, and Mom could still pull towels and sheets and underwear through the hand-fed wringers. About 1978, Great Aunt Rose and Great Uncle Bud sold us their used washer and dryer. After all, they still worked. Incredibly, they were still running in 2014, the year Mom moved off the farm.

And near the laundry was the basement drain. A good thing, because the basement leaked. Just a trickle, and only after a hard rain, but it leaked nonetheless. That trickle started in the center of the south wall, ran down that wall, and then sidewinded its way under the pool table. It continued under the staircase, finally coming to an end at the basement drain.

Dad's bar was just a few steps from the drain. On the bar, there were puzzles and games, like "Liar's Dice," which consisted of an old cigar box and five dice inside. A player shook the box, cautiously opened the lid, then announced the results of the shaken dice. "Two pair." "Three of a kind," and so on. The dice had to match or beat the previous player's roll, or the next player could call you out. If you were caught lying, you were done. If they accused you and you were innocent, they were out.

Dad's bar was full of life lessons.

Just to the right of Dad's bar stood shelves and shelves of records—country albums and big-band recordings, LPs and 45s, Dad collected them all. We grew up hearing Jo Stafford sing about shrimp boats and Jim Reeves welcoming us to his world. Gene Autry told the story of Rudolph every Christmas morning, and Les Brown and His Band of Renown welcomed each New Year with "Auld Lang Syne."

No, we never finished the basement, but we filled it with fun and lots of love, just as it was.

31

ALL THE WORLD'S A STAGE

I'VE BEEN a bit of a clown from the start.

At least, on stage.

I made my stage debut as Jack-in-the-Box. I was in Mrs. Boglo's third grade class, and she'd chosen a play about a shopkeeper and a set of toys that come alive as a class project. We were all given assignments: classmate Dawna Brewer played an old woman, Mark Blom may have been a soldier, and I was a clown.

Rehearsals must have gone well. I remember staying still and quiet in the box until it was my turn, and I recall popping out and saying something clever and funny— perhaps even the line written for me in the script.

On the day of the performance, I was excited. I was scared. Well, excited and scared and unable to stay still in the magical wind-up box. I jiggled. I jostled. And I finally jumped up and said something. My line got a laugh, and while no one was surprised that there was a boy in a box, I was hooked.

In my next major elementary-school production, I portrayed Benjamin Franklin, inventor of electricity. I had the breeches, the kite, and a rather large key. I had no lines.

I'm sure the performance was, uh, electrifying.

Fast forward to my senior year at Highland High School and a student-directed show appropriately titled *Bits and Pieces*. The production highlighted songs and dances from Broadway shows, including *West Side Story, Pippin,* and *42nd Street*.

Jeff Guetensberger sang the opening number, the title song from *42nd Street*, while the rest of the cast crossed the empty stage behind him, each time a different character: shoppers, businessmen, moms pushing baby strollers, cops on the beat.

Now, to make things easier and perhaps more "theatrical," our director asked each of the players to dress in black. The guys wore slacks, the gals in matching wrap-around skirts that tied at the waist. That's an important plot point, so pay attention.

"...to the avenue I'm taking you to..." It was time for my final cross. I'd been a businessman late for an appointment, a sailor seeking feminine company, and now I was a thief, about to lift the purse from an unsuspecting Lisa Brusack.

"*…naughty, bawdy, gawdy, sporty…*" I took a deep breath, made my dash, and grabbed Lisa's purse—and the tie that held her wrap-around skirt.

Up went her hands. Down went her wrap. And utterly unaware of why her staged scream seemed more real during tonight's performance, I continued to dash across the stage, dragging Miss Brusack along with me.

"*…42nd Street!*" The number ended, the applause—and laughter—erupted, and the show went on.

I was still hooked. But perhaps a life in the theater wasn't exactly for me. I should choose something safe, more substantial, more secure. Where I could make a decent wage, work regular hours, and not be concerned about costume malfunctions.

Like farming.

Or teaching.

32

PUT BUBBLES IN YOUR WATER

BABIES HAVE CHUBBY CHEEKS. And moms and aunts and grandmas like to pinch those cheeks and make original comments, like, "Look at those chubby cheeks!"

Charming.

Except when you're five, or seven, or, in my case, twelve, and your mom, your aunt, and your grandma are still saying, "Look at those chubby cheeks." At least no one was still pinching me at my thirteenth birthday party, except for my Aunt Kathy. My "favorite aunt," as she calls herself, could get away with murder, then and now. Around that same birthday, she had me stand on the front porch of the "new" house while she cut my hair. Shaving the back of one's head at an angle never caught on. Thank goodness my hair grew quickly back then.

My elementary school classmates were pretty normal kids, which means we all picked on and teased one another. No one was bullied, or perhaps everyone was. It was a different time. Nonetheless, I gave them plenty of material to work with: eyeglasses with soda-bottle bottom lenses, a speech impediment, many pairs of fat-kid jeans with "Husky" on the brand label. (Husky Buske. Why, Mom, why? Couldn't we afford Levi's or Wrangler or even Toughskins?)

And my cheeks. My chubby, chubby cheeks.

A family trait, my father said. Wear them with pride.

I proudly wore them on the school bus, and when another kid made fun of me, I punched him. It was the only time during my public-school education that I was called to the principal's office. I enjoyed my lunches in Mr. Nichols' office the rest of that week.

By middle school, I was no longer "the fat kid with the Coke-bottle glasses."

Now I was "Bubbles," a nickname a neighbor kid gave me one long morning bus ride from the farm to Highland Junior High.

Lovely.

Soon, everyone called me that. Even my friends. Even some of my teachers.

"Aren't you the kid they call "Bubbles"?

"Yes, ma'am, but I prefer Mark."

After almost two years of this, uh, teasing, I decided to embrace my popular moniker and run for election. The school announced that they'd partnered with the City of Highland to teach us about the various positions folks held in city management: mayor, police officer, fire chief, and so on.

I ran for water commissioner. My slogan: "Put Bubbles in Your Water." No kidding. Handmade signs hung everywhere in the halls of Highland Junior High. I actually said it as the closing line of my persuasive speech, which I delivered to the entire eighth-grade student body gathered in the old high school auditorium.

Guess who won and got to take part in the one-day field trip around the city? Yours truly! Take that, you skinny kids with high cheek bones and contact lenses! For one day, Bubbles ruled.

I grew taller, thinner, and lost the requisite braces on my teeth. My elementary and junior-high years were behind me, but I couldn't shake the nickname. While most of my friends had stopped referring to me as Bubbles, the rest of the world had not. So I hung with my band buddies, my choir companions, and the drama geeks. I wrote for the school paper, went to German club meetings, and endured a lot of, uh, teasing in the locker room of the boy's gym.

Fast forward to the end of senior year. I'd sung the lead in a review of *Pippin* and danced with the cast of *Bits and Pieces*, a musical review. I was cast in the chorus of *The King and I*, which called on all of us to dye our hair black, praise Buddha, and dress in period-appropriate costumes.

When all the shows were over, Ms. Hill, the drama director, held a sort of cast party for seniors only, and I was excited to attend.

One by one, Ms. Hill drew each of us aside during the party and gave us a small gift. Mine was a bottle of bubbles, the kind with the screw-top lid and the little plastic dipper you're supposed to dip in and blow through. Her final dramatic direction to me: "Use this to blow 'Bubbles' away, then get a fresh start in college."

I blew the bubbles as directed, and sobbed like a small, chubby-cheeked child. And I chose education over water management. Teaching would afford me the chance to positively impact students, perhaps as much as Ms. Hill's directions had impacted me.

33

CHRISTMAS IN THE NEW HOUSE

IT WAS PROBABLY 1976 when we put up our last "live" tree. By then, we'd been in our new home for two years, and the living room had a plush gold and green shag rug. We'd chosen a particularly tall and wide evergreen; it was too big for the tree stand and so gangly that Dad tied it up to curtain rods on one side and the front door hinge on the other, just to keep it upright.

One day, a vacuum-cleaner salesman stepped into the front room with just a little too much enthusiasm. Down went the tree and out went the salesman.

Mom didn't buy a new vacuum, but she did buy an artificial tree the following year.

∾

THE KITCHEN CLOCK-RADIO clicked on each morning at 6 a.m. The station was KMOX, and the announcers were Rex Davis and Bob Hardy. I'd stay in bed until 6:30, listening for school closings and to the daily "Dime Rhyme." Then I'd give up, get out of bed, and get ready for my school day.

What's a dime rhyme? A poem, sent in by listeners. If the poem was read on the air, Mr. Davis and Mr. Hardy sent you a dime. I know this because, as I lay in bed one December morning, the hosts read a poem I'd sent in. They announced my name as the author, and later sent me a congratulatory letter with a dime taped to it.

And what was the topic of the poem? What else? Wishing for a snow day!

THE ANNUAL SUNDAY School Children's Christmas pageant was a pretty typical affair. Every year, Sis dressed as an angel, I was a shepherd, and the older kids played the roles of the kings and the holy family. That is, until I signed up for band at the elementary school and started playing the drums. Then I became the annual drummer boy.

When I started, Mom asked the band director if I could practice in the barn, rather than in the house. By high school, I played snare drum in the marching band, concert

band, and pep band, though I still wasn't allowed to practice in the house.

I was welcome to practice in the barn, though. Dad liked
to hear me play. He once hired me and a keyboard player
to entertain for his annual New Year's Eve party—a small
gathering of twenty to thirty of Dad's closest friends. That
party was a success, and since I never had a date for New
Year's Eve—and could also play the keyboard—I became
the one-man band entertainment for the next few years.

I played polkas, schottisches, and waltzes, some slow two-
step tunes, and all the requests I could manage.

Never once was I asked to play "The Little Drummer Boy."

MOM ALWAYS LOVED POINSETTIAS. One year, Dad
brought home one of these Christmas wonders and hid it
out in the well house, a small building that housed a well
and a refrigerator, but no heat source.

Anyway, Dad clearly never saw the old *Frosty the Snowman*
animated special; if he had, he would have known that
poinsettias should be kept in a hot house, not an unheated
well house. By the time he brought that poor thing in, well,
let's just say Mom was really surprised.

A WORKBENCH. That was what was in the big box, the last present I opened one Christmas morning. Not a racetrack or a game or even new clothes. A workbench. My childhood was over. I was disappointed and probably did a crummy job of hiding that feeling. But that workbench—and a jigsaw—were soon put to work, as I traced old patterns that were once Aunt Erna's on to plywood, sawed them out, and placed them in our yard.

I got better with practice, and soon ran out of room in our yard. So I used paper feed sacks to draw Santa and elves and nativity figures. I cut out the figures, attached a framework so each would stand on its own, and got creative with many colors of outdoor paint.

I'd sell these original creations at local craft shows, county fairs, and church bazaars. I made just enough of a profit to cover my expenses and saved the remainder for college.

As it turned out, that old workbench was a great Christmas gift after all.

"PRETTY PAPER, PRETTY RIBBONS OF BLUE." Dad would sing those old lyrics every Christmas morning as we unwrapped our gifts—objects wrapped in pretty paper, then concealed in gift bags, cookie tins, and Famous-Barr boxes used and reused from prior holidays.

We were a thrifty lot and tended to give each other useful items, like toothpaste and cans of peaches. No kidding. One year, Sis and I received matching toilet plungers. Another Christmas, we found matching step stools under the tree.

The most memorable and perhaps unusual Christmas gifts were the matching cemetery plots. Our folks had purchased burial plots for themselves earlier that year and figured they might as well buy one for each of us. Mine is beside Dad's, on the end of the row—a good thing, since I'm the tallest in the family. I'll need the most leg room....

IN THE WINTER OF 1982, there was snow in the lane, over the fields, and piled deep along the highways. Schools were closed, churches were shuttered, and all business stopped for days.

At one point, we lost power on the farm; we spent three days using the camp stove to cook our meals. We moved food from the refrigerator to the red cooler with the white lid, then kept the cooler outdoors in the snow.

We slept side-by-side in sleeping bags on the carpeted living room floor. We played card games inside, built igloos outside, and threw hay down from the lofts for the cows.

It was a wonderful time of family togetherness. Of all the memories I've shared, this one remains my favorite.

PART III

A HANDFUL OF STORIES FROM MOM
AND DAD

My folks, Dolores and Vernon Buske, at Camp Chaffee,
Arkansas, April 1954

34

GROWING UP DAD

Now that I've shared stories of my growing-up years, I thought it only fair to let my folks share some of their own growing-up stories. These memories are told from their perspective, gleaned from stories written down by Dad in his later years, and conversations I had with Mom after Dad passed.

~

But first, a quick introduction:

Vernon Edwin Buske was number nine in a family of ten kids. He was born in 1932, the year Franklin D. Roosevelt replaced Herbert Hoover as President of the United States and four years after the start of the Great Depression.

He was raised on a farm about equal distance from Troy and Edwardsville, Illinois, though he always considered

Troy his home. He attended a one-room schoolhouse—
Maple Grove School—which, despite his claims to the
contrary, was located just at the end of his farm's lane. In
other words, a short walk to and fro, and neither journey
was uphill.

Many of his stories still resonate with me today, perhaps
because I see so much of myself in him, and also because of
the times in which we're currently living.

Now, here's my dad, Vernon, in his own words…

35

LIFE ON A FARM IN THE 1930S AND '40S

SOME OF MY earliest memories are of Dad working with horses. We farmed with only horses until 1946, when he purchased a small Farmall B tractor. That was Dad's pride and joy, and he used to rest it—to cool down the motor—after two or three rounds in the fields.

I remember as a very small child, I walked behind Dad once as he plowed with a two-horse walking plow. I only remember that one time, because Dad replaced the walking plows with riding plows. A one-bottom 16-inch plow was called a sulky, a two-bottom 12-inch plow was called a gang plow. I remember how proud I was the first time I got to drive three horses, riding that sulky plow.

Over the years, I learned to harness the horses, hitch them to equipment, drive to the field, and work the ground for planting. To pass the time in the field, I'd sing every song I knew. We listened to country & western music on the radio, and I'd memorize all the verses.

And I learned how to plow, disc, and harrow. The harrow was dangerous; we stood on a board for weight and had to jump off at every row's end.

We had four horses: Jim, Babe, Silver, and Bally. Bally was almost blind, and you had to talk him through ditches and around fences.

Our house was a two-story farmhouse. We had no electricity or running water. Our lights were kerosene lamps, and our water was drawn from a well, using a chain and an oak bucket. Mom would also use the well to cool milk cans and other food we didn't want to spoil. As for the kerosene lamps, our eyes grew accustomed to the light; when we went to the neighbors who had gas lamps or even electricity, the lighting was so bright it almost hurt our eyes.

We had two stoves—a kitchen range and a heating stove in the living room. Mom cooked on the range, so we kids had to go out to pick up corn cobs and kindling wood for her. Dad hauled dead wood from a neighbor's timber and sawed it with a hacksaw. That wood was used in the heating stove.

I remember Mom cooking pancakes for all of us. If we didn't have syrup, or oleo, or sugar, we ate our pancakes with hot milk poured on top.

Milking was done by hand. Mom and the kids did most of the milking. The milk was strained into cans and kept cool in the well, then picked up daily and taken to the Edwardsville Creamery.

We raised pigs from the sows and sold them when they were fat. We butchered hogs for meat and Mom would fry it down or cold pack it in jars so that it would keep all year. No electricity also meant no freezer.

Along with the pigs, we had forty to fifty laying hens and would collect the eggs every day. Once a week, we would sell twelve to fifteen dozen eggs at twenty to thirty cents a dozen. That would give Mom enough money to buy whatever groceries we didn't grow ourselves for a week.

And every spring, Mom would set several hens on eggs to hatch. Those newborn chicks would replace the older hens that had died or were butchered and give us some young roosters to eat.

I often joked that there are five kinds of people: city people, town people, country folks, poor folks, and Buskes. But we never thought of ourselves as poor. We had enough, and we had each other. That was all that mattered.

36

SCHOOL DAYS

Maple Grove was the name of our school. It was a one-room school building with all eight grades together. There were less than twenty-five people in the entire school, all taught by one teacher. We read aloud to each other and did our numbers at the blackboard in front of one another. The school year lasted eight months and was over by the end of April. Then we could go back to farming.

We lived just a short distance from school and walked home every day for lunch. Mom would sometimes send me to school the year before I was old enough to start. I would sit at a desk in the back, and the teacher would let me color or just listen.

I don't remember learning to read. I just remember loving to read even before starting school. The Edwardsville daily paper had a comic section that featured Alley Oop, Major

Hoople, and Captain Easy. I loved reading about the adventures of Buck Rogers and Red Ryder.

In first grade we had four students: Clyde Spitze, Ruth Ackerman, Joyce Dull, and me. The next year it was just Joyce and me. Clyde Spitze was held back, and Ruth Ackerman transferred to the Lutheran school in Troy. From that point on, Joyce and I competed for the highest grades; she usually won. Her mom, Wilma Dull, would substitute for our regular teacher from time to time. She would always pray before we started. She had no training in teaching, but we enjoyed having her there.

Every day we would say the Pledge of Allegiance while facing the American flag—that was before the words "under God" were added. While saying the pledge, we would extend our right hand, palm up, toward the flag. That changed during World War II. The German salute (Heil Hitler) was somewhat similar, so we started placing our hands over our hearts instead.

After the pledge, we would sing a few songs. Some teachers graded us by how loud we could sing. Maurice Dull got better grades than me, and he couldn't even carry a tune.

Recess was ten or fifteen minutes in the morning and again in the afternoon. We played games like Kick the Can, Handy Andy Over, and Run Sheep Run. When the teacher rang the bell, recess was over, and it was back to reading and math.

Once a month, we would be tested on what we had studied. The tests would come from Edwardsville and were taken by everyone in the county. And once a year, usually in the fall, we would skip some of the regular lessons and practice songs, poems, skits, and plays that we'd memorized or written ourselves. These were presented at the annual Box Social; all the parents were invited to attend.

After the entertainment was over, there was an auction. Many of the moms brought cakes and pies, and they were sold to the highest bidder. Usually, things sold for a dollar or two, not very much.

And some of the girls would bring decorated boxes with sandwiches, cookies, or snacks of some kind. The boy who purchased the box got to share it with the girl who brought it. No one was supposed to know which box was brought by which girl until after it was sold and opened, and the girl's name was discovered inside.

I remember one young man who started bidding on the box his date had brought. There was a small group of guys who decided to bid against him and kept bidding him up. He finally prevailed, but paid about twelve dollars for the decorated box and the right to share its contents with his date. Twelve dollars! That was a fortune!

After the auction, we all shared in a light meal and went home. Everyone felt good about the evening, especially those of us who took part in the entertainment. Everyone was already thinking about next year.

Everyone, that is, except the teacher. I am certain that she was very glad it was over!

37

MY FIRST JOB

I GOT my first real job in the summer of 1942. I was almost 10 years old. It was for Fred Buesking, working with the baling crew. My brothers Les and Elmer worked for him already. Bob Kreutzberg was the other member of our baling crew. Together, we baled straw for many of the neighboring families who couldn't afford their own equipment. My brother Melvin worked for Charlie Bangert, another farmer.

We worked with an Ann Arbor portable baler. It had its own motor and Fred pulled it with an Allis-Chalmers tractor. The baler motor started with a hand crank, as did the tractor. One of the guys drove the tractor while the other two rode on either side of the bale chute. One would poke wires into the bale while the other tied them off, then one of them would place wooden blocks between the bales.

I was too little to mess with any of that. It was my job to stand on a board on the front of the baler at just above the entry point of the straw. There I used a pitchfork to help guide the straw into the bale chamber. It was hot, but easy work and I was paid two dollars per day.

The best part of the day was after work when we'd stop at Marie's Tavern. Mr. Buesking, brother Les, and brother Elmer would all get beers. I would drink an ice-cold Pepsi. Mr. Buesking would let me drink Pepsi, but not eat any candy bars. They were not good for me.

After we finished baling straw bales, we'd start baling straw stacks using an Ann Arbor stationary baler. We would move to a farmer's straw stack, Elmer would pitch the straw on a platform, and Bob Kreutzberg would feed it into the baler. Now I would poke the wires and Les would tie them. Les would also stack the bales; I was too little to lift them.

The work lasted until I went back to school. That fall, I started fifth grade. Our teacher was Mr. Bartlett, the only male teacher I ever had. He tried to get Joyce Dull and me to skip fifth grade completely and go to sixth, but Mrs. Dull would not let that happen!

When the weather turned cold, Mr. Bartlett gave me my second job. He asked me to fire the furnace in the basement of our one-room school. I went to school early in the morning and would go in on Sunday evenings. He paid me five cents per weekday and ten cents per Sunday.

I hated going in on Sunday evenings as I was afraid to go into the spooky basement alone. Whenever possible, I convinced my sister Arlene to go with me.

I was very happy when spring came!

38

THE WAR YEARS

THE YEAR WAS 1940. Hitler was moving across Europe. All four of my grandparents had immigrated from Germany and they were following the news probably more than most.

I remember Dad listening to our one and only battery-operated radio. He would listen to Hitler's speeches, then listen to the local newscaster's interpretation. Sometimes, he would hit the table and say, "That's not what Hitler said." He was not a sympathizer, but Dad and his brothers thought Germany got a bad deal after World War I.

By late November, we were butchering hogs. Some of the neighbors were helping. Mr. Spenser, our mailman, delivered the mail about 10:30 every morning. In the mail that day was an induction letter for brother Melvin. He was to report in December for one year of service. Mom shed a tear, but Melvin was ready to go.

Melvin was sent to Camp Pendleton in California. He had one furlough in mid-summer and would complete his one year of service in mid-December, but the Japanese attack on Pearl Harbor on December 7 changed that. Melvin served as a medic in the Pacific Theater, taking part in numerous island battles. He didn't come home until 1945.

World War II changed the lives of all Americans, including us Buskes.

Rationing started. We got a small amount of gas, which we used in the car since we didn't have a tractor of our own. Car tires were almost impossible to get. I learned to drive in a 1946 Chevrolet. I was just twelve years old, but I drove all over the place. Since we had no spare, I learned to take the flat tire off, patch it, then pump air into it and put it back on.

I grew up fast.

The war dragged on. Every day we would look through the *Edwardsville Intelligencer* for news of the battles. My cousin, Kenneth Landolt, was listed as missing in action in Africa. We drove to Grantfork to console Aunt Till and Uncle John. Aunt Till cried and then gave me one of Kenny's toys, a metal airplane about eighteen inches long. I thought it was great, but broke it trying to sail it through the air.

Several months later, we found out Kenny was a prisoner of war, held in a German camp. He spent the balance of the war there.

Cousin Delmar Rosenthal was wounded in the Battle of the Bulge. Cousin Harold Brunsworth came home unscathed. Neighbor Art Young came home shell shocked and was never the same.

Brother Melvin received the Bronze Star for action in the Pacific. He would never tell me what happened, but I would sneak up when he and his buddies would get together. I'd try to listen and hear their stories, then I'd tell what I heard to Maurice.

Maurice Dull and I were good friends. Before the war broke out, we played cowboys and Indians. During the war years, we played soldiers, and when no one was around, we would smoke Dad's pipe, which wasn't a good idea. Sometimes we would find Dad's Redman or Days Work chewing tobacco. That was an even worse idea.

On September 27, 1946, I turned 14. By then, the war had been over for about a year. During the war years, I'd learned to drive a car and drive the neighbor's tractor. I'd finished eighth grade and didn't go on to high school; Dad said I didn't have to if I didn't want to, and I didn't want to. I wanted to be a farmer.

By that time, brother Elmer had married Henrietta Heman and brother Les had married Eileen Gilomen. My sister Erna had married Erwin Smith, and sister Leona had married Eldon Prott. Norma, Melvin, Arlene, and I were still at home, but not for long.

39

CHRISTMAS IN THE '40S

Christmas at our house was not a huge event, although we looked forward to it like everyone else. At school, we made Christmas cards and gifts, carving things out of soap bars. It was easy to carve a dog or a bird.

On Christmas Eve, Mom and the kids would go to church. The Sunday School classes would always give a pageant and we would take part. We made our own costumes and carried Grandpa's walking stick. After church service, they gave us a small box of hard candy and we headed home.

At home, Dad had been busy. He put up the same artificial tree we always used. The toys would be under the tree, usually one wind-up toy, some candy, and clothes. The tree would have some real candles, which Dad would light. It was beautiful when we blew out the kerosene lamps and the room was dark.

That was the only time they were lit, as there was danger of starting a fire. Dad always said Santa Claus brought the tree, but we knew he couldn't come down the chimney as both stoves were in use—and it was always the same tree.

Christmas morning, we would come downstairs and start putting together and playing with the toys we got. One Christmas, I got a bicycle under the tree. It was used and in pieces, but my brothers put it together and I still have the bike today. I'll bet I rode a million miles on it.

After dinner, someone would have to clean the cowbarn and prepare for the evening milking.

The cows didn't care if it was Christmas.

40

GROWING UP MOM

DOLORES MARIE HOFFMANN was number one in a family of six kids. She was born in 1934, two years after the introduction of Franklin D. Roosevelt's New Deal, smack dab in the middle of the Great Depression.

She would always call the city of Highland, Illinois, home, but had no affection for one address over another, except perhaps the caretaker's house, a white frame home on the grounds of Lindendale Park. Her folks moved the family— by then there were five kids—into that home in 1947.

Mom was thirteen at the time and had lived in at least seven other homes her parents had rented. She was working at Highland Hospital, where she wasn't a favorite of Sister Ferdinand, and soon she'd graduate from the eighth grade of St. Paul's Catholic school.

Mom didn't share many of these stories until after Dad passed, and only then while she and I watched television when I came to visit. Frankly, during their 60-year marriage, I'm surprised she had the chance to share any stories at all. She was always busy baking cookies, or zucchini breads, or pies, and Dad was a talker.

Now, here's my mom, Dolores, in her own words…

41

ALL AROUND THE TOWN

MOM AND DAD were living in White City, in a little house not far from the coal mine, when I was born. That area was, and still is, considered part of Highland, and I never did know why it was called White City. Anyway, we moved just down the street soon after, close to the brewery. The Metzgers, my paternal grandparents, lived just on the other side of the alley. Mom said if she couldn't find me, I was over playing with Rose and Isabelle. Rosie and Izzy were Dad's half-sisters and technically my aunts, but they weren't much older than me and liked to dress me up.

We were always moving—sometimes it was because the house we were renting sold, sometimes it was because Mom was expecting another baby and we had to move to have more space. And sometimes we moved if Dad lost his job or found a better one.

Over the years, he worked as a night watchman and as a bus driver. He worked at the shoe factory and ran a gas station. Dad helped Mom run the Snack Bar across from the Lory Theater and, after that, the Broadway Grill, which was just off the city square on Broadway. Once, the TV show "Route 66" filmed an episode in Highland and used Broadway Grill to film a scene. Dad was paid a single dollar for that.

After the house by the brewery, we lived upstairs in a house on Eighth Street, just down from the First Congregational Church. We still went to Mass at St. Paul's, but I went to Girl Scout meetings at First Congregational. I had more fun there.

For just one summer, and for a part of that fall, we lived where Highland Silver Lake is now. Then, that valley had a bunch of houses—shacks, really. We didn't have running water or electricity that summer, and my brother Don and I had to walk to St. Paul's elementary school. That meant walking from our house in the valley up "ten-minute hill" and then all the way across town.

It took ten minutes for a horse and wagon to get up the hill, that's how the hill got its name. It took us a lot longer to walk to school. Don would sometimes hitch a ride with the milkman and pretend he didn't know me. Brothers!

We moved a number of times after that. By the time we moved to the caretaker's house at Lindendale Park in 1947, there were five of us: me, Don, Kenny, Kathy, and Richard. The youngest, Tom, was born six years later.

The house had five rooms and electric lights, but no running water and not much else. Outside was a two-seater toilet, garage, coal storage bin, water well, pig pen, chicken coop, and space for a garden.

Dad had signed a twenty-year lease, agreeing to serve as the custodian and manager of the park. Dad had a steady job, and there was plenty of room. Now we finally had a place to call home.

42

LIFE AT THE PARK

FROM THE START, we kids were all part of the "crew." Our jobs included mowing the park grounds, cleaning the dance hall and park restrooms, and picking up litter, especially glass soda and beer bottles. We would take our coaster wagons, run over the park, pick up bottles, and sometimes find money. We probably looked harder for coins than we did for bottles.

As we got older, Dad gave us new jobs, usually connected to the events held at the dance hall. Now we were coat checkers, ticket takers, money counters, cooks, and bartenders. We iced down soda and beer and kept as many as four separate park buildings stocked, depending on what type of event was going on. Company picnics, county fairs, city fireworks displays for the 4th of July—there was always something going on.

About 1956, Dad and Uncle Bud built a set of concession stands, square wooden buildings painted white with dark brown trim. (Bud, which is what we called my Uncle Leo Grotefendt, had married Dad's sister Rosie in 1942, but kept it a secret from the family until the fall of 1943.) The first stands were down the hill by the stock car races, and there we sold sandwiches and coffee as well as popcorn and snow cones.

In those days, school picnics were held at the park. Dad bought the first cotton-candy machine in the area, and kids would stand in long lines to spend a dime on cotton candy or a nickel on popcorn.

And on top of all of this, I attended school at St. Paul's and worked part-time at Highland Hospital. It was 1946, I was 12, and Mom gave me a note to give to the Sisters at the hospital. It said, "Please give Dolores a job, and keep a part of her wages to help pay our family's bills." I worked in the kitchen, carrying trays of food to patients, and worked after school and weekends through eighth grade.

I didn't go on to high school. School was not for me, as the nuns reminded me constantly. The nunnery wasn't for me either, though St. Paul's sent us girls on a bus to visit the convent in O'Fallon, Missouri.

I moved to full-time at the hospital after graduation and stayed until I'd had enough. Sister Ferdinand—we girls called her "Ferdinand the Bull"—blamed me for whatever went wrong.

One day, I heard a crash on the dumbwaiter downstairs and from where I was, all the way upstairs, I could hear Sister Ferdinand yell my name.

I quit. Walked right out and went home. Walked into the kitchen, ready to tell Mom I'd quit and realized I was fifteen and didn't have a job. So, I turned around, went right back out, and got a job as a waitress.

It didn't pay much, and I quit a week later. I found another waitressing job closer to home.

It was hard work, but I no longer had to put up with Sister Ferdinand's bull.

43

GOOD CATHOLIC GIRLS

ONCE IN A WHILE, Aunt Cleda would send me a dollar in
the mail, along with the invitation to visit her and stay
overnight. Cleda married Kenny Parker; they lived in St.
Louis, so I'd use the dollar as bus fare and ride over to
Grand Avenue. There, we'd go shopping or see a movie at
the Fox Theater.

Sometimes I'd go over with a bunch of girls, and we'd get
off the bus near Forest Park. We could spend the day at the
zoo, or at the Highlands Amusement Park, and ride the bus
back to Illinois—all on our own.

Mom and Dad took us to the Highlands a couple of times.
It was near Forest Park, close to where the St. Louis Science
Center is now. It had rides and concessions, but mostly we
walked around and looked at the fun house mirrors, the
penny picture shows, and other free stuff.

Mom always packed a picnic lunch and Dad always drove. He was deathly afraid of bridges and would sweat bullets and swear like a sailor when we crossed the Mississippi. We kids would sit in the back seat and make fun of him.

I remember on one shopping trip to St. Louis, I bought a new dress. It was the latest style, and I brought it home and modeled it for Mom. When I turned around, she saw the cut-out in the back. Mom made me take it back. "Good Catholic girls," she said, "do not wear dresses like that."

Not long after, I met Vernon. It was 1951, and he was working at the Alton Box Board factory in Highland; his sister, Norma, and his brother, Elmer, also worked there. Anyway, I was at the company Christmas party with my Aunt Tootie, Mom's sister. Her real name was Bertha, but everyone called her Tootie.

Near the end of the party, Vernon came over and asked Tootie if he could take her home. She wouldn't go with him. He didn't ask me.

A year later, we met again. This time at a dance held at Diamond Mineral Springs in Grantfork. Earlier that year, I'd been to the movies with a farmer, and I could smell the stink of a farm on his clothes. I swore I'd never go out with a farmer again. Vernon asked if he could take me home after the dance that night. I said yes. If I'd known then he was a farmer, I would have said no.

He asked me to marry him soon after and gave me an engagement ring for my nineteenth birthday, November 14, 1953.

44

LIFE AS AN ARMY WIFE

VERNON and I had been engaged for about five months when he got the draft notice. The Korean War was winding down, and he was living with his mom and dad, helping them farm. I had moved back in with my mom and dad after a short attempt to be on my own, renting the upstairs rooms of a house on Broadway in Highland. My roommate got married to a guy I used to go with, and I couldn't afford the rent on my own.

Anyway, Vernon reported for induction on April 5, 1954. He was assigned to Camp Chaffee, Arkansas, where he was in basic training for ten weeks. When his two-week furlough came up, I rode down with Vernon's folks in order to bring him home. One of his Army buddies, Harold Gilomen, was also coming, so Harold drove our 1948 Plymouth. Vernon's dad rode in the front, and Vernon, his mom, and I rode in the back. It was a long ride home.

Things moved fast during those two weeks. Vernon's brother Melvin married Doris Jean Federer. Now his folks had little help running the farm, which they rented from Fred Dzengolewski, a farm Vernon wanted to move back to once we were out of the Army. And he received his next orders from the Army: electronic school at Ft. Monmouth, New Jersey, part of the Signal Core. We decided I'd join him there and we'd get married on base.

I asked his sister Arlene to be my maid-of-honor. My own sister, Kathy, was barely ten years old. Arlene was only two years younger than me, and the two of us got on a train in Highland and rode overnight to New Jersey. We were so excited when we arrived that we left our hats on the train.

Vernon was waiting for us at the station. He'd been up all night, not allowed to sleep on the train station benches. The first thing he asked me was if I had any money. He didn't have enough to cover the cab fare back to the base.

We were married by an Army chaplain. Vernon asked Alfred Carl, who he'd met back in basic, to be his best man. It was just us, Arlene and Al, Vernon and me, the organist and the chaplain.

The organist had already started playing when the chaplain noticed that our marriage certificate was short one signature. Al said he'd drive really quick to the Justice of the Peace and get it signed. He was back ten minutes later; the organist was still playing, and we completed the ceremony.

To this day, neither one of us is really sure who signed our marriage license.

Our wedding reception, if that's what you want to call it, was at a place off-base Vernon found for us—a small house in Redbank, New Jersey, which we shared with another Army couple, Merle and Bobbie Dodson from Texas. Just a few of the guys from the base came over for drinks. Our landlord told us, "No wild parties," but he was the only one who drank too much that day.

Vernon continued with electronic school, building tube radios from scratch, and I got a job as a waitress at Mr. Ponti's Greek restaurant. Mr. Ponti and his staff were good to me, though they made fun of that Illinois girl who ordered "weenies and beans." All the food they served was different than what I'd helped Mom fix back at Lindendale Park. I suppose you could say it was all Greek to me.

After eighteen weeks of electronics school, they took some of the top students and sent them to Aberdeen Proving Ground for advanced training on the M33, a 90mm cannon. Vernon didn't make the cut.

After twenty-one weeks, the Army picked a second group and sent them to Aberdeen Proving Ground. This time, Vernon made the cut and we were moving again.

We had moved to Oceanport, New Jersey, to our own place after a few months with the Dodson's. Now we were moving again, this time to an apartment in Havre de

Grace, Maryland. We weren't there long, and moved yet again, this time to a house we shared with yet another Army couple, Dave and Joan Sorvig. We now lived just off the base in Aberdeen, Maryland.

After almost a year in service, Vernon finished his schooling and was assigned to Fort Bliss, El Paso, Texas. Once again, we packed what little we had into a 1948 Pontiac and drove, first back to Illinois to see our folks, then on to El Paso. We drove straight through, each of us driving in turn.

We made it to El Paso and started looking for a home. We stopped at a real-estate office and talked to a Mr. Wilcox. It was a lucky stop, because he had a two-room house next to his that he rented out. We drove to his home and talked to Mrs. Wilcox. They asked for $60 a month. The house was small, but nice and quiet, so we took it. We now lived on Rose Lane in El Paso, Texas.

Vernon reported to his new unit, part of the 161st Ordinance Detachment, a small unit of about twelve specialists servicing the T75 cannons that guarded big cities across the U.S. His pay covered our rent, so once again I found work, this time at Van Horn's bakery. The job was fun, and the pay was alright, but the best part was that I could bring home cookies and donuts that didn't sell.

My mom and dad drove out to see us, bringing my little brother Tom along. We all stayed in our two-room home, and Vernon and I went with them to see White Sands, New Mexico.

One weekend, we crossed the Rio Grande on the walking bridge, entering Juárez, Mexico. It cost one penny to cross into Mexico and two pennies each to cross back. While there, we saw a bullfight that was bloody. I didn't think too much of that.

In March of 1956, Vernon got a letter from Fred Dzengolewski, saying that there was a dispute over money—fifty dollars, if I remember right—and could Vernon come home to take over the farm? Otherwise, according to the letter, Fred would kick Vernon's parents off the property.

I didn't want to go. I never wanted to be a farmer's wife, and while things weren't perfect, life in the Army was good. But Vernon wanted to be a farmer, so...

Saying goodbye was not as easy as we thought. We had made some real friends, lifelong friends who we stayed in touch with through phone calls, Christmas cards, and occasional visits the rest of our lives. But we packed and took a longer route home through northern New Mexico, Colorado, Kansas, and Missouri. Back to Illinois. Back to the farm.

Back home.

PART IV

ALMOST HOME

Dad, me, Sis, and Mom, back on the farm.

45

LIFE IS WHAT YOU MAKE IT

VERNON AND DOLORES, my parents, came home from the Army and moved in with Grandma and Grandpa Buske in May 1956.

Dad would turn twenty-four in September; Mom, twenty-two two months later. Their second wedding anniversary wasn't until August. Time, which had flown while they were stationed on the East Coast and "out in the west Texas town of El Paso," now moved slowly.

Farming was rough in the early '50s. St. Louis saw a record 115-degree day in July of '54. Repeated droughts devastated wheat, corn, and bean fields. Grandpa and Grandma Buske survived on egg money from the chickens, milk money from the cows, and job money earned by Dad's sister Arlene, who was still living at home.

And now my parents were living there, too.

Dad's thoughts:

"It didn't take long to adjust to civilian life. We farmed together with Mom and Dad for about one year. Then they retired and we bought their machinery and the livestock.

"I started agricultural school at Highland High School under the G.I. bill. I built up a line of machinery. I had Dad's SC CASE tractor and I bought an old C Model CASE tractor. It never had a starter, so we had to hand crank it.

"Fred Dzengolewski owned the farm we were renting, and he and I got along very well. He loved coming to the farm as Dolores always fed him coffee and cookies, or he would eat with us if it was lunchtime. She was a very good cook.

"Mom and Dad moved on to cousin Larry Prott's house, a farmstead near Marine, for a short time. When Larry married and moved in, Mom and Dad moved out and into a rental house just behind our church, then known as Marine Evangelical and Reformed, now known as Marine United Church of Christ.

"Sadly, Mom passed away in October 1958. Dad passed just three weeks later. There was money from the sale of their furniture to cover Mom's funeral, but the eight of us kids split the cost of Dad's arrangements. I had to borrow my portion from the bank.

"Now we were really on our own. Eventually, Fred sold us forty acres, then ten more. When he died in 1968, his widow Evelyn gave us the chance to buy the remaining acres. We agreed, and now farmed 170 acres and were deep in debt.

"It didn't take too many years to figure out that it was hard to make a living just farming. We sold the dairy herd and raised hogs and beef cattle instead, but after the money from the G.I. bill stopped, I knew I had to do something else. I knew if I got a job, Dolores would have to quit her full-time work at the restaurant. She wouldn't be too happy about that."

Mom's thoughts:

"Those people did everything different. They milked cows morning and night. They worked but never seemed to get ahead. Grandpa went to church while Granny stayed home to watch wrestling.

"And they ate different things. Pork liver. Head cheese. Gooseberries. Cold-packed beef. She canned tomatoes and everything else that grew in the garden. My Mom didn't cook like that, so I learned to do these things from Granny.

"I also learned to eat supper before I got home from work.

"I worked full-time for my mom and dad, first at the Snack Bar, right across from the Lory Theater in Highland. Then Mom opened Broadway Grill, and I worked there.

"My salary wasn't much, but I put it in a jar in the kitchen, which is where Granny kept the egg money and where Arlene put her salary, until she married John and moved out. I didn't like it, but that's the way it was.

"We didn't have any furniture of our own, so we slept on an old iron-framed bed in one of the two upstairs bedrooms. That room was on the north side of the house, and it was always cold.

"After Vernon's folks retired from farming and moved to Marine, we started making the place our own. We bought a deep freezer, then a china cabinet from a widow in Troy. Cost us $5. One year, we bought a living room set, a black couch, and chair, and Grandpa—my Dad—bought an orange leather swivel chair to go with it. I spent three months lying on that couch, pregnant with you. That's another story.

"Vernon farmed and I worked for my mom until about 1961. That spring, Vernon got a job driving an oil spreader for Bituminous down in Collinsville. He expected me to stay home and take care of the livestock. Let's just say I wasn't too happy about that.

"That first spring on our own, I followed Vernon out to the fields with the second tractor and helped plow. After a bit, he waved me over and told me I wasn't doing it right. We went back to plowing, and he waved me over again. This time, he wasn't so nice about telling me I was doing it wrong. The third time he waved me over, I showed him. I drove the tractor back to the house and went inside.

"I didn't mind feeding the pigs or cleaning the chickens. I didn't mind keeping the garden or canning peaches. Vernon liked my cooking. And he never asked me to work in the fields again."

46

THE RIDE QUEEN

ON ONE HAND, Dad was devoted to the fields, carefully preparing the soil in order to plant wheat, beans, and corn. He cultivated the young plants, prayed for rain during droughts, and reaped the bountiful harvests at the close of each year.

On the other hand, Mom was devoted to the lawn.

Well, mostly to *mowing* the lawn.

Initially, it was just Mom and a used Lawn-Boy mower. She'd set us kids on the front porch, tell us to play and stay there, then push the little mower over the grass. There were small patches that needed to be cut at the front and to the south of the old farmhouse. The tract to the west was larger; the wash line hovered over the middle of that area. Mom didn't have to mow the north side; there, a hedge row ran the length of the house, covering the septic tank and a section of pasture fence.

In other words, it didn't take her long to mow what served as our lawn.

When I was deemed old enough, it was Mom and Sis who sat on the porch, keeping a watchful eye over me, making certain I didn't run over Mom's new flower bed or, more likely, my own foot.

Then something wonderful happened. We got a riding lawn mower—a Ride King, straight from Hamel Tractor Supply! Suddenly, the sky was the limit, or at least the hog lot fences were. I continued to push the Lawn-Boy about, but now Mom could ride out to the wide-open spaces—the grassy knolls around the tool shed and out by the south barn.

Soon Sis was taking her turn with the push mower, and Mom and I traded off the other assignments—shaving the tall grass near the hog barns, the machine shed, and the chicken house.

We built the new house just five feet from the old one, then tore the old one down and covered the basement with dirt and sod. Voila! More lawn to mow.

By this time, mowing the lawn was a full day's work. We mowed around the horseshoe pits, between the corn cribs, and down both sides of our long country lane—all the way out to Route 4.

The farm never looked so good.

One day, I bypassed the grape arbor, steered clear of the swing hanging in the apricot tree, and then ran right over the new walnut tree saplings Dad had gotten from Uncle Eldon. I hadn't cut off my foot, but it was back to the push mower for me.

That meant Mom could dash about on the riding mower once again. I think its top speed was two miles per hour.

Now, on one particular sunny afternoon, Mom was on the rider working a plot of grass that stretched from the apple tree to the vegetable garden, when I saw her wave both arms above her head.

I shut off the Lawn-Boy.

"Snake," she cried, and waved some more. "Get a hoe."

I ran to the well house, where the garden tools were kept, and grabbed a hoe. She was driving in circles as I ran toward her.

"I hate snakes!" she yelled again. She slowed enough to grab the hoe from my hand, then proceeded to wave it above her head. For one fleeting moment, she looked like the Wicked Witch of the West, about to kill Toto.

"Got 'em!" Mom said with a grimace. With the snake balanced on the blade of the hoe, she walked to the pasture fence and flung it over.

"I think I'm done for today. Can you finish up?"

I was promoted back to the rider, which is where I stayed for years.

And as for my mom, she was happy to return to her work indoors and let her two teenagers handle the lawn mowing. She only got back on that horse after we'd grown up and moved away. Long after Dad had retired and stopped working the fields, Mom was still keeping most of that three-acre "house place" tidy and trim.

Not a single snake ever dared again to outrun the queen enthroned on her Ride King.

47

DAD ON A HOT TIN ROOF

ANY NUMBER of images come to mind when I think of my dad:

- Dad sitting next to the auctioneer, serving as clerk at another Saturday farm sale, as I ran the sale sheets to the company clerk.
- Dad tossing a softball my way, letting the door to the well-house serve as a backstop as I swung at the air.
- Dad steering the combine through the dry bean fields as I rode beside him in the dusty cabin.

But maybe, just maybe, the clearest picture I have of Dad is one I never saw: Dad strapped to the toolshed roof, paint brush in hand, the ladder lying flat on the ground below.

Let me explain.

Paint was Dad's solution to most problems, at least when it came to keeping the farm looking sharp. The barns were painted every five years or so, a rusty "barn red," typically by some fly-by-night troop that drove up the lane and offered a deal Dad couldn't resist.

He had me paint the hog lot and pasture fences the same color, though those buckets of oil-based lacquer were less watered down than what was used on the barns. I tried to get as much on the fence posts as I got on myself, and I usually succeeded.

And once a year, Dad handed Sis and me giant brushes and a bucket. I've never understood why, but the trunks of our maple trees sparkled white with fresh paint every spring, thanks to our efforts.

In his retirement, Dad discovered Bob Ross and the joys of painting landscapes. He also discovered spray paint, and combined his two new interests. Suddenly, his horseshoes were bright orange and the horseshoe pegs, silver. The little white cabin by the farm pond now appeared to be built of brown logs, complete with a fake window and Dad's version of a cowboy peering out of it.

He created wood cut-outs of bears, spray-painted them, and hid them in the woods behind the house. And, thanks to Bob Ross, he painted a landscape on that well house door, complete with a black 'v' in the blue sky—a "happy little bird."

Which brings me back to Dad strapped to the roof.

Dad was almost eighty years old when he got it in his head that the tin roofs of the chicken house and the tool shed needed a fresh coat of paint. He tackled the first with ease over a couple of days; the chicken house was barely a story tall and within view of the kitchen window. In other words, Mom could keep an eye on him as he painted and she baked another rhubarb pie.

The tool shed, though—that was a different animal. It was two stories at its peak and tucked farther away from the house and Mom's watchful eye.

Making things worse, Mom had run into town on some errand, and wasn't home when Dad decided to wrap himself with a strong rope and anchor his 5-foot, 8-inch frame to the top of the tool shed.

He slipped. The ladder fell. And there he hung, half on the roof, half on the side of that "barn red" barn, nowhere to go and no one to get him down.

Like I said, I wasn't there. But I can sure see him hanging around, waiting for Mom to come home.

She did, of course, come home and heard him calling, "Dolores! Hey, Dolores!" from where he hung.

Nothing was hurt, except maybe his pride. After that, he stuck with respraying the bears and painting landscapes.

Each with a "happy little bird."

48

A CUT ABOVE

To ME, butchering day didn't look much different in the 1960s and early '70s than it did to my Dad in the 1940s and early '50s. We did most of the same things in the same manner, except Dad talked about the neighbors all pitching in. In my early years, it was mainly the uncles and aunts helping out.

We did the same for them, spending many cold and wet March Saturdays at Uncle John's or Uncle Gerp's or Uncle Les's. Of course, at Uncle Les's, it was more about the amount of beer that was consumed than the amount of work done.

Not that I was old enough to join in the drinking, nor was I big enough to do much of the work—at least, not at first. Butchering day was, for Sis and me, a chance to play with our cousins, eat our share of the cakes and pies the aunts had baked, and listen to the stories Dad and his brothers and his brothers-in-law told. Those stories were always about the way they used to do things.

Here's how my dad remembers butchering day:

"Butchering was a long, hard day but we all looked forward to it. Some of the neighbors would come over to help. It started several days before: gathering wood, setting up kettles, and preparing crocks to store the meat.

"On butchering day, Dad would be up by 4 a.m.; he'd light the wood under the large kettles, then fill them with water. The rest of us would help with the daily morning chores while Mom fixed breakfast. With eight kids, and most of us at home, she always had a tableful to feed.

*(The actual acts of butchering were not, and still are not, for the weak of stomach. *Warning: specific descriptions follow.)*

"About 6:30 a.m., some of the neighbors would arrive to put the finishing edge on their knives. By 7 a.m., Dad would shoot two hogs.

"The other men would stick the hogs and collect a portion of the blood, which was later used for the blood sausage.

"The hair was removed from the hogs with scalding water. They were then hung from branches for a good cleaning and the rest of the process. Some parts were removed for later use, or immediate use such as the liver, which Mom prepared for our noon dinner. Everyone liked fresh hog liver, especially with mashed potatoes, milk gravy, stewed tomatoes, and homemade pie.

"Casings were cleaned and soaked in salt water to be used for sausage making later.

(*In later years, prepared casings were purchased from a butcher shop in Troy, which simplified at least that part of the process.*)

"After lunch, the four quarters of each hog were cut into hams, bacon, and shoulders. The trimmed meat would be separated, the fat from the lean. The lean would be ground, mixed with salt and pepper, then stuffed into casings. That was pork sausage. The fat was put into a black kettle, boiled down, then stored in large crocks. That was lard.

(*Mom never could make her pie crust taste the same once we stopped butchering. Lard makes the best crust!*)

"Other parts of the hog which were cooked earlier were ground, mixed with seasonings, and also pumped into casings. That was liver sausage. Some of that meat was set aside, ground, seasoned, and mixed with the collected blood. That was blood sausage. Head cheese was also prepared with scraps from the… well, you know.

(*Dad always said he failed me in three ways. He didn't teach me to cuss, to like beer, or to eat blood sausage. Once I observed the process, is it any wonder why?*)

"Everyone that helped would get a sample.

"The next day, Mom would slice and fry down the hams and shoulders so we could store them in the cellar. We'd hang the bacon in the smokehouse to cure. That would give us meat to eat all summer."

(And that, as they say, is good eatin'!)

49

I'LL DANCE AT YOUR WEDDING
FOR THAT

UNCLE ELDON often said this to me when I was a kid: "I'll dance at your wedding for that." I didn't think much of it at the time, but I asked Mom what he meant years later.

"It's something people said if you agreed to do them a favor," she explained. I don't recall doing any favors for Uncle Eldon, though I helped out around his farm whenever Dad had me in tow, so I guess I heard "I'll dance at your wedding..." often.

Mom and Dad didn't have a fancy wedding. They married on base at Ft. Monmouth, New Jersey, and the reception, if you can call it that, was a supper given by a few friends back at the house they rented with another couple. And there was no wedding dance for Uncle Eldon—or anyone else—to enjoy.

So, when their twenty-fifth wedding anniversary approached, Dad insisted they throw a big dinner and dance to celebrate. "After all," Dad was known to say, "it's been the twenty happiest years of my life." (In later years, he changed that line to thirty, and then forty, as they approached their fiftieth and then sixtieth wedding anniversaries.)

August 14, 1979, was the official date for the party and planning began a full year before. They booked the Alhambra Township Hall, which was large enough to hold 300 of their closest family and friends. Everyone who was invited showed up, and from the crowd I recall, I suspect a few party crashers did, too.

They hired "Company," a local dance band that could play a mean polka, a traditional waltz, and all the current country tunes. I don't think Dad cared what they played, as long as he and Mom got to start and end the evening with, "a belly rubber," otherwise known as a slow dance.

Mom designed, baked, and decorated the cake. She spent hours hand-piping yellow roses, each one created separately with a rose petal-tipped icing bag, then frozen on sheets of waxed paper.

Mom, Sis, and I carried that multi-tiered cake out of the basement, placed it in the car, and then ever-so-slowly drove it to the Township Hall. How we got it out of the car and reassembled on the display table without dropping it, I'll never know.

The caterer delivered fried chicken, roast beef and gravy, and the requisite mostaccioli, the most mispronounced pasta dish served only at receptions in the Midwest. Mom's mom was in charge of green beans, potato salad, and whatever other sides were served. Her sisters-in-law brought extra desserts to slice and serve.

Dad made arrangements for the beer.

It was a heck of a party, and certainly made up for the celebration they never had back in 1954.

But the real story happened after the party was over.

About twenty to thirty of Mom and Dad's closest family and friends followed us home, bringing the leftover food, the leftover beer, and the largest of the gifts Mom and Dad received—an oil drum, cleaned up and painted silver. "Happy 25th Dolores and Vernon" was hand-lettered in red on its side, a big red heart on its top.

There was plenty of noise-making—a "chivaree," they called it—followed by the decision that Dad needed to dance with Aunt Eileen in the middle of Illinois Highway 4, the main road at the end of our long farm lane.

As the whole crew walked out to the highway, we sang a chorus of a polka titled, "In Heaven There is No Beer," and we took pictures of Eileen and Dad attempting to dance.

Once we were all back by the house, someone decided to open that silver oil drum and dump the contents across the garage floor. Sawdust, coins, and horse manure spilled out. Everyone laughed and laughed and laughed some more. Dad removed the dried manure, and eventually everyone removed themselves and went home.

Things grew even more unusual the next day. Grandma and Grandpa came out, as did Great Aunt Rose and Great Uncle Bud, and we began to clean up the sawdust pile.

Sis and I held squares of chicken wire over five-gallon buckets, while Dad and Uncle Bud shoveled the sawdust into the buckets. The coins, scattered throughout the pile, were caught by the chicken wire, while the shavings fell through to the bottom of the buckets.

Then Grandma and Mom ran a hose over the coins, rinsing off the dust and any remaining manure, and laid them out on old tablecloths to dry. Aunt Rose collected the coins in granite tubs, the ones we usually used for making sausage, and Grandpa started rolling the coins in paper rolls.

All told, almost $500 was there—in pennies, nickels, and dimes, with a few quarters tossed in for good measure. It took days to roll them all, and Mom said that when she carried the rolls into the bank in the granite tubs, the teller's eyes grew wide.

So, if you do me a favor, "I'll dance at your wedding for that." In return, I'll do a favor for you sometime, as long as it doesn't involve sawdust, coins, or horse manure.

50

PRESS ON!

A LONG, long time ago, in the days before wrinkle-free material, folks ironed. Well, moms ironed. At least, my mom did.

Nothing got past Mom's hot iron. Shirts, slacks, pillow-cases, tablecloths—they all were steamed or starched or pressed under Mom's diligent hand, which was guided by her watchful eye.

A twelve-inch black-and-white television kept her company. It sat on a slender wire stand on wheels, what today's designers might call mid-century modern and what my mom would have called "on sale" at the Highland Freight Salvage store.

Mom passed a lot of hours ironing our clothes and listening to "One Life to Live," "All My Children," and "The Mike Douglas Show." Mr. Douglas later gave way to

Miss Dinah Shore, who hosted her own variety daytime talk show. Soap operas were a guilty pleasure, and Dinah's show featured Hollywood stars from Mom's teen years.

Nothing really changed when we moved into the new house, except now those afternoons were spent in the basement. Freshly pressed shirts were hung on exposed water pipes between the floor joists above. Mr. Douglas and Miss Shore competed with Donny and Marie, and Mom still stopped all work at 3 o'clock to fix herself a cup of instant coffee. I think that's when "Days of Our Lives" came on.

Through my middle school, high school, and even my college years, Mom continued to iron my shirts, slacks, and handkerchiefs. Freshly pressed clothes magically appeared in my closet, which I rifled through each morning, searching for the right outfit for the day.

One day, Dad came into my room, opened the closet bi-fold door, and said, "It would please your mother if you hung all your shirts facing the same way." I rifled no more and remembered to thank Mom for her hard work.

I was still living at home, and Mom was still washing and ironing my clothes when I started my first teaching job at Triad High. When I finally moved out, she bought me an iron, an ironing board, and a bottle of spray starch—Faultless Heavy Finish. I dutifully pressed my Kmart slacks and shirts for work, but arrived at the annual Buske family reunion that September in casual, unpressed clothes.

I learned of Mom's displeasure through my cousin Sharon. "Dolores says you've got your own apartment now, and that she got you an iron for a housewarming gift. Guess you'll have to learn how to use it."

Message received.

I still iron my handkerchiefs with Mom's old iron, and I still use Faultless spray starch—$1.27 at Walmart. I also press my own dress shirts and hang them, each facing the same way, in my closet. I'll keep being thankful for what my parents, and everyone around me, do for me every day.

And I'll press on.

51

ONE CHRISTMAS EVE

My folks were newly married and living in Aberdeen, Maryland, in 1954. Dad was serving in the Army, Mom found work as a waitress in a little Greek restaurant.

Neither of them earned a lot of money, but they wanted to come home for their first Christmas together. So, Dad bought a well-used car for $350. He found two Army buddies who wanted to share the ride to Illinois, and plans were made—drive all night, drop the guys off, and head home to Mom's family in Highland, and Dad's folks on the farm near Alhambra, Illinois.

Things didn't go according to plan.

They ran out of gas.

The engine overheated. Not just once, but several times.

Mind you, this was 1954. Eisenhower didn't authorize the interstate system until two years later. People communicated by writing letters. They needed coins to make phone calls, and public phone booths were few and far between.

Not much help for four young travelers driving through the night, just to get home for Christmas.

It took them thirty-five hours—in other words, they fed water and gas to that old junker through the first night, all the next day, and into the second night. They dropped the guys off, and finally pulled up to the old farmhouse at 1:30 a.m. I imagine Granny and Grandpa Buske were sound asleep by then.

At this point in the story, I'm reminded of Mary and Joseph, trying to get to Bethlehem. No, Mom and Dad weren't expecting. Their first kid—me—didn't arrive until ten years later. And I don't think the donkey that carried Mary broke down as often as that old car did. But still, the parallels are there. A long journey. The desire to be warm and welcomed. The need to be home.

The story doesn't end there.

Mom wrecked that car a few days later. She was headed out to Uncle Les's farm, ran off the road, hit her head on the windshield, and busted her ankle. It could have been worse, though Christmas on crutches could not have been fun.

The car didn't fare as well. It was junked, and Mom and Dad had to borrow $300 to buy a used Plymouth to get back to Maryland. Dad's leave would be up soon. Fifty of those dollars came from Grandpa Hoffmann. Mom said they paid her dad back a little at a time.

But they'd made it home.

EPILOGUE

"What did you learn from your dad?"

It was the first question the Pastor asked me when he met with Mom, Sis, and me to gather some information for Dad's eulogy.

I wasn't sure how to answer.

Six years later, that same pastor asked me almost the same question. "What did you learn from your mom?"

I was no more ready with an answer than I was for Dad.

Putting these pages together, placing these memories on the page, grieving their loss and celebrating their lives...these things helped me finally answer that pastor's question.

- To drive a tractor and work the fields.
- To hit the ball and enjoy the game.

- To work harder than the next guy.
- To save money for a rainy day.

But more importantly…

- To treat folks like you want to be treated.
- To find something positive in everything and everyone.
- To save room for dessert.
- To never meet a stranger.

My folks gave me a large dollop of little moments, a lifetime of stories and memories. I've learned that I'm a little more like them every day, and for that, I'm thankful.